SPECTRUM

Writing

Grade 5

Published by
Frank Schaffer Publications®

Frank Schaffer Publications®

Spectrum is an imprint of Frank Schaffer Publications.

Printed in the United States of America. All rights reserved. Except as permitted under the United States Copyright Act, no part of this publication may be reproduced or distributed in any form or by any means, or stored in a database or retrieval system, without prior written permission from the publisher, unless otherwise indicated. Frank Schaffer Publications is an imprint of School Specialty Publishing. Copyright © 2007 School Specialty Publishing.

Send all inquiries to:
Frank Schaffer Publications
8720 Orion Place
Columbus, Ohio 43240-2111

Spectrum Reading—grade 5

ISBN 0-7696-5285-9

1 2 3 4 5 6 POH 11 10 09 08 07 06

Table of Contents Grade 5

Table of Contents, continued

Chapter 5 Write to Persuade

Chapter 6 Write to Explain

Chapter 7 Write to Inform

Chapter 1

NAME ______________________

Lesson 1 Find Main Ideas and Details in Pictures

A picture has a **main idea**. The main idea is what the picture is all about. Circle the sentence below that tells the main idea of this picture.

Fishing requires certain equipment.

Many fish are being caught.

Fishing is a popular hobby.

A picture also has **details**. Details are the little parts that make up the whole. For example, one detail in this picture is that the man has a fishing net. Another detail is that the tackle box is open.

Write some more details from the picture.

The setting is in a lake or the ocean There are no fish in the lake of ocean at the time.

Lesson 1 Find Main Ideas and Details in Pictures

What is this picture all about? Write the main idea here.

____

Write some of the details in the picture here.

_______________________ _______________________

_______________________ _______________________

_______________________ _______________________

Now that you have looked at the separate parts of the picture, put them together. Write a paragraph about what is happening in the picture. In your paragraph, use the main idea and some of the details you recorded.

____

____

____

____

____

____

____

____

____

NAME ____________________

Lesson 2 Find Main Ideas and Details in Text

My dad was always happy when he was fishing. At the lake, he was endlessly patient. I don't know how many times he taught us to cast. There were also all the times he had to wade out and unsnag our hooks. He never complained.

Like a picture, a paragraph has a main idea. The main idea is what the paragraph is all about. In most paragraphs, the main idea is actually stated in the paragraph. That statement is called the **topic sentence**. A topic sentence may be anywhere in a paragraph, but it is usually either the first sentence or the last. In the paragraph above, the topic sentence is the first sentence. Underline it.

In the paragraph below, the writer did not include a topic sentence. Read the paragraph. Then, write a topic sentence below the paragraph.

The local fishermen have been trying to catch him for years. They've been telling stories about him for years, anyway. They have nicknamed him "Puss-in-Boots." They tell of a catfish so big that they fear their boats would tip if they ever did hook him. Their stories place him anywhere from two feet to 12 feet long. Everyone agrees on this, at least: a very large fish lives in Lantern Lake.

____

____

You already know that the details in a picture are the little parts that make up the whole. In a paragraph, details tell about, or support, the main idea, which is stated in the topic sentence.

Look back at the paragraph at the top of this page. Remember, the first sentence is the topic sentence. Each sentence that follows is a detail that supports the idea that dad was always happy when he was fishing. List several details from that paragraph here.

____

____

____

____

____

____

____

____

NAME ______________________________

Lesson 2 Find Main Ideas and Details in Text

Read the paragraph below. In it, the writer shares her memories of fishing. Find the topic sentence and underline it. Then, list some details that support the main idea.

My uncle went out in his rowboat almost every morning. When he had guests, he enjoyed the company in his boat. He was also glad to be alone again after they left. My aunt and uncle enjoyed the fresh fish he caught. He never seemed disappointed when he didn't catch anything, though. His pleasure came from fishing, not from catching fish.

Details:

____

____

____

____

Now, read this paragraph about water safety. Underline the main idea. Hint: It is stated in one part of a sentence. Then, list some details that support the main idea.

Most people are glad to spend a day at the beach. What some people forget is that water safety takes some extra thought. Boaters must check weather reports ahead of time. They must also make sure their equipment is in good repair. They also must have life preservers for all passengers. Swimmers should always swim with a buddy. Even strong swimmers should never swim directly away from shore. They should also rest for 15 minutes for every hour in they are in the water.

Details:

____

____

____

____

NAME ______________________

Lesson 2 Find Main Ideas and Details in Text

What do you know about fishing? Choose one of these sentences as a topic sentence for a paragraph:

I don't know much about fishing.

I know a lot about fishing.

I went fishing once, and the memory of it is a (good/bad) one.

Now, write a paragraph in which you support your main idea with details. Remember to choose just one topic sentence.

____

____

____

____

____

____

____

____

____

____

Now, make up a fishing story about "the one that got away." In a paragraph, tell about that fish that you saw but never hooked, or that you almost caught. When you are finished, underline your topic sentence.

____

____

____

____

____

____

____

____

____

NAME ____________________

Lesson 3 Staying on Topic

Most of the details in this picture fit the main idea, but one does not. What is it? Describe the detail that does not fit.

____

Now, write a sentence that states the main idea of the picture. Remember to ignore the detail that doesn't fit.

____

Normally, all of the details in a picture fit the main idea. The same should be true of a paragraph. All of the details should fit the main idea. That means that each sentence must stay on topic.

Here is a good paragraph. It starts out with a topic sentence. Then, each sentence gives details about, or supports, the topic sentence.

On my way to school, every block is different. First, there is the house block. Each house has a driveway and a grassy front yard. Then, there is the office block. Each doorway has a sign on it, and I always wonder what is behind the doors. The third block is the store block. The stores have big glass windows, and I can see myself as I walk by. Finally, there is the playground block. It is the school's playground, and I look through the fence to see which of my friends are already there waiting for me.

NAME ______________________

Lesson 3 Staying on Topic

Each of the following paragraphs contains a sentence that is not on topic. Read each paragraph. Underline the topic sentence. Draw a line through the sentence that does not support the topic sentence. Then, list four details that support the topic sentence.

The courthouse in our city is made of great big limestone blocks. Those blocks came from a quarry just outside of town. Beside the old quarry is where the first mayor lived. When the courthouse was built in the 1870s, limestone was chosen as the building material because it was nearby. Teams of horses pulled carts from the quarry to the building site. Each cart had just one big limestone block on it.

Detail: ______________________

Detail: ______________________

Detail: ______________________

Detail: ______________________

Long ago, people built their homes with whatever was handy. People who lived in forests built shelters out of sticks, limbs from trees, or logs cut from tree trunks. I was in a log cabin once, and it was made out of huge logs. People who lived in hot places where there were few trees made the walls of their homes out of mud. On the Plains, people cut blocks of sod and stacked them up to make the walls of their houses. People who lived in cold, snowy lands learned to dig into a snow bank or to build a house out of blocks of snow.

Detail: ______________________

Detail: ______________________

Detail: ______________________

Detail: ______________________

NAME ____________________

Lesson 4 The Writing Process

Good writers follow a plan when they write. They take certain steps that make up the writing process. Following these five steps leads to better writing.

Step 1: Prewrite

This is the time to discover and plan. Writers might choose a topic, or they might list everything they know about a topic already chosen. They might write down what they need to learn about a topic. Writers might make lists that contain complete sentences or just words. Some writers might begin to put their ideas in order by making a chart or diagram.

Step 2: Draft

Writers put their ideas on paper. This first draft should contain ideas that are written in sentences and organized in paragraphs. Good writers keep their prewriting ideas nearby. There will be mistakes in this draft, and that's okay.

Step 3: Revise

Writers change or fix their first draft. They move ideas around, put them in a different order, or add information. They make sure they used clear words that really show what they mean. This is also the time to take out ideas that are not on topic.

Step 4: Proofread

Writers usually write a neat, new copy. Then, they look again to make sure everything is correct. They look especially for capital letters, end marks, and words that are not spelled correctly.

Step 5: Publish

Finally, writers make a final copy that has no mistakes. They are now ready to share their writing. There are many ways for writers to publish their work.

NAME ____________________

Lesson 4 The Writing Process

Pam used the writing process to write a paragraph about a fantastic vacation. Her writing steps, below, are out of order. Label each step with a number and the name of the step.

Step ___: ____________________

The most exiting vacation spot I can think of is the South pole. I think it would be very cool to learn how to make an igloo. Then, of course, I would sleep in it. I would use lots of blankets. ^Then I would wake up cook pancakes over a little fire right there in the igloo. Just to stay in touch, I would take along my own person satellite and laptop so I could send daily reports ^to my family by e-mail.

Step ___: ____________________

The most exciting vacation spot I can think of is the South Pole. I think it would be very cool to learn how to make an igloo. Then, of course, I would sleep in it. I would use lots of blankets. Then, I would wake up and cook pancakes over a little fire right there in the igloo. Just to stay in touch, I would take along my own personal satellite and laptop so I could send daily reports to my family by e-mail.

Step ___: ____________________

South Pole vacation
igloo
lots of blankets
fire for cooking
satellite

Step ___: ____________________

The most exiting vacation spot I can think of is the South pole. I think it would be very cool to learn how to make an igloo. Then, of course, I would sleep in it. I would use lots of blankets. I would wake up cook pancakes over a little fire right there in the igloo. Just to stay in touch, I would take along my own person satellite and laptop so I could send daily reports by e-mail.

Step ___: ____________________

The most ex^citing vacation spot I can think of is the South Pole. I think it would be very cool to learn how to make an igloo. Then, of course, I would sleep in it. I would use lots of blankets. Then, I would wake up and cook pancakes over a little fire right there in the igloo. Just to stay in touch, I would take along my own person^al satellite and laptop so I could send daily reports to my family by e-mail.

NAME ____________________

Lesson 5 Purposes for Writing

When you are in school, many of the things you write are school assignments. You write them because your teacher has asked you to do so. Beyond completing a school assignment, though, there are several basic purposes, or reasons, for writing. Generally, they are:

- to entertain
- to persuade
- to explain
- to inform

Writers use many **forms** of writing, such as friendly letters, reports, news articles, book reviews, and poems. Here are the purposes for writing, along with the forms of writing that writers can use.

Purpose for Writing	Forms of Writing
To entertain	stories, poems, plays, personal accounts or narratives, humorous articles or essays, friendly letters
To persuade	letters to the editor, business letters
To explain	how-to instructions, eyewitness accounts
To inform	reports, news articles, book reviews, friendly or business letters

Writers may combine purposes in one form of writing. For example, a writer may both inform and persuade in an article about the importance of saving the rainforests.

Below is a list of written products. Write what you think the purpose of each item was—to entertain, persuade, explain, or inform.

Written Product	**Purpose for Writing**
instructions for planting seeds	____________________
a letter to the editor about an upcoming election	____________________
a retold fairy tale	____________________
an article about the school play	____________________

NAME ____________________

Lesson 6 Audience

When a band performs a concert, an audience listens. The band director chooses music that the audience will enjoy. For example, the band would not play very serious music for an audience of children. Likewise, they would not play "Mary Had a Little Lamb" for a group of college students.

After a writer writes, the audience reads. A writer needs to think just like a band director does. Consider these questions:

What will my audience enjoy?
What are they interested in?
What will make them want to keep on reading (or listening)?
What do they already know?
What will they understand?

In addition to thinking about why you are writing, you must think about your audience. Like the band director, you do not want to present something that's too serious for your audience. You also do not want to present something that is too simple.

Here is a paragraph about planting trees. A man who owns a tree nursery wrote it for a group of young children. He forgot to think about his audience. Read the paragraph. Then, ask yourself the five questions above and write how the paragraph should be changed to meet the needs of the audience. Suggest specific changes.

Dig a hole twice the width of the tree's root ball. The depth should be about the same as the root ball. Put in the appropriate fertilizer or soil supplements. Set the tree in the hole. Have someone support the tree while another person backfills the hole. Mulch to within two inches of the trunk. Water thoroughly.

____

____

____

____

____

____

____

____

NAME ______________________

Lesson 7 Write a Paragraph

Here is what you know about paragraphs.

- A paragraph is a group of sentences that are all about the same topic.
- Each sentence in a paragraph tells about, or supports, the paragraph's topic. In other words, each sentence stays on topic.
- The main idea of a paragraph is what the paragraph is all about.
- A paragraph's main idea is usually stated in a topic sentence. The topic sentence may fall anywhere in the paragraph, but is often the first or last sentence.
- The first line of a paragraph is indented.
- Writers must consider the audience for which they are writing.

Your teachers want to hear your opinion about the best part of school. Maybe you think it is the kids, teachers, computer lab, or the new football field. Complete the topic sentence below. Then, list some reasons for your choice.

The best thing about my school is ______________________________.

Reasons:

______________________ ______________________

______________________ ______________________

______________________ ______________________

Review your list. Think about the order in which you want to present your reasons in a paragraph. Then, draft a paragraph about what you think is the best part of your school.

____

____

____

____

____

____

____

____

NAME ____________________

Lesson 7 Write a Paragraph

Read through your paragraph. Ask yourself the questions below. Make changes to your paragraph and rewrite it below.

____

____

____

____

____

____

____

____

____

____

Questions to Ask About a Paragraph

Does the topic sentence express the main idea?
Does each sentence support the topic sentence?
Does each sentence express a complete thought?
Are the ideas, words, and language appropriate for the audience?
Is the first line indented?

Now that you have thought about the content, or meaning, of your paragraph, proofread it for errors. Read the sentences several times, looking for a certain kind of error each time. Use this checklist.

____ Each sentence begins with a capital letter.

____ Each sentence ends with the correct punctuation (period, question mark, or exclamation point).

____ Each sentence states a complete thought.

____ All words are spelled correctly. (If you're not sure, check a dictionary.)

Now, rewrite your paragraph on a separate sheet of paper. Use your neatest handwriting and make sure there are no errors in the final copy.

Chapter 2

NAME ____________________

Lesson 1 Personal Narrative

Have you ever written a true story about yourself and what you did? You were writing a personal narrative. A personal narrative is a true story an author writes about his or her own experiences.

Tanner wrote a personal narrative about going to work with his mom.

Shadowing Mom

School was cancelled today because the furnace broke. Mom didn't want me home by myself, so she took me to work with her. She is the Activities Director at a senior housing center. It's a place where older people live. Mom says they aren't sick, but they just couldn't keep up the homes they used to live in.

I figured I would just sit in her office and read. Mom had other ideas. Right after we got there, she announced that I would be the caller for the Thursday morning Bingo game. I knew better than to complain, but inside I was screaming. I'm way too old to play Bingo!

There were about 15 people in the dining room waiting to play. They were all talking and laughing. Mom introduced me and helped me get the game started. They all paid attention, even though there was still some talking and laughing going on. They got me to talk and laugh, too. They were teasing me about being too young to play Bingo. Now, that's a laugh!

Spending the day with those people made me realize that people with gray hair aren't just old people. They are funny, full of life, and still interested in the world. They made me feel very welcome. I wouldn't mind going to work with Mom again some day.

Here are the features of a personal narrative:

- It tells a story about something that happens in a writer's life.
- It is written in the first person, using words such as *I, me, mine,* and *my*.
- It uses time and time-order words to tell events in a sequence.
- It expresses the writer's personal feelings.

NAME ______________________________

Lesson 1 Personal Narrative

Why do people write personal narratives?

They might want to share their thoughts and feelings. They might want to entertain their readers. Often, people write to share their experiences *and* to entertain.

Who reads personal narratives?

If you write a personal narrative, teachers, parents, and classmates might read it. As you think about your audience, ask yourself what you want to share with your readers. What might they learn about you?

What can personal narratives be about?

They can be about anything that actually happens to the author. It might be a happy or sad event, a silly situation or a frightening one.

So, what could you write a personal narrative about? Here are some idea-starters. Look them over.

the earliest holiday I remember
my first sports practice
my greatest accomplishment
the thing that makes me angry
my first day of school
the best family trip
my most embarrassing moment
my biggest challenge

What memories popped into your head as you read these idea-starters? Jot some notes about each memory. One of these could be the start of a great personal narrative!

Idea-starter: ______________________________

____

Idea-starter: ______________________________

____

Idea-starter: ______________________________

____

Idea-starter: ______________________________

____

Idea-starter: ______________________________

____

Idea-starter: ______________________________

____

NAME ________________

Lesson 2 Time Order

In a personal narrative, readers need to know when things happen and in what order. Understanding the order of events helps readers put other ideas together, such as why something happened or what meaning an event had. That is what **time words** are for. Think of all the time words or phrases you can, and list them. Here are some ideas to help you get started.

after lunch	Monday	at dawn
yesterday	last week	October
____________	____________	____________
____________	____________	____________
____________	____________	____________
____________	____________	____________

Now, use some of the time words you listed. Write a sentence that could be from a personal narrative. Use a time word or phrase at the beginning of your sentence.

____

____

Write a sentence about something you did recently. Use a time word or phrase in the middle or at the end of your sentence.

____

____

Write a sentence about something funny or odd that happened to you. Use a time word or phrase at the end of your sentence.

____

____

NAME ______________________

Lesson 2 Time Order

In addition to time words, transition words help readers know when things happen and in what order. Here are some common transition words.

after	as soon as	before	during	finally	first
later	meanwhile	next	soon	then	when

Here is a paragraph that uses some transition words. Circle the transition words when you find them.

During homeroom, my name was called over the loudspeaker. I was supposed to go to the office. As soon as they heard it, my classmates gave me a hard time about being in trouble. My face was about as red as my sweater. When I got to the office, the principal had a really funny look on her face. She went to the window and pointed. Then, I knew what it was all about. My dog had followed me to school. He was sitting right beside the sign that read, "No pets, skateboards, or motorized vehicles on school grounds."

Use some transition words in sentences. Combine them with time words from the list on page 20 if you like.

Write about something that happens in the evening.

____

____

____

Write about two things that happen at the same time.

____

____

____

Write about three things that happen, each one after the other.

____

____

____

Lesson 3 Active Voice

Usually, the subject of a sentence does the action. That is easy to see in this sentence:

Germaine pitched the ball.

The verb in the sentence is an **active verb** because the subject does the action.

What about this sentence?

The ball was pitched.

First, is this a complete sentence? Yes, it is. It has a subject and a predicate. *Ball* is the subject of the sentence. Does the ball do the action? No, the ball does not do the action; the ball "receives" the action. The verb, *was pitched,* is a passive verb because the subject does not do the action.

Passive verbs are always two-part verbs. There is always one of these helping verbs—*am, is, was, were, be, been*—plus a main verb. Does that mean that whenever you see one of those helping verbs, you are looking at a passive verb? No!

Passive verb: Germaine was motioned to the dugout.

Active verb: Germaine was motioning to the manager.

How can you tell the difference? Ask yourself these two questions:

What is the subject?

Is the subject doing the action?

If the answer to the second question is "yes," then you have an active verb. If the answer is "no," you have a passive verb.

Sometimes, passive verbs must be used. Maybe what did the action is not known: "A run was scored." Most of the time, however, writing will be clearer and more interesting when writers use active verbs.

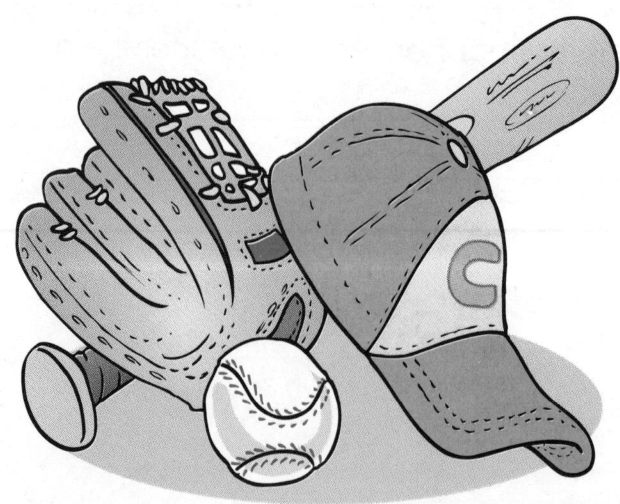

NAME ____________________

Lesson 3 Active Voice

Compare these two paragraphs. The one on the left is written mostly with passive verbs. The one on the right is written with active verbs. What do you notice?

The first game of the season was won by the Carver Colts baseball team. The first four innings were pitched by Jacob Harrell. Tim Moya was called in as relief pitcher by manager Hal Wells. Hits were made by four Colts team members. Runs were scored by just two of them, Shane Ranson and Mario Miranda.	The Carver Colts baseball team won the first game of the season. Jacob Harrell pitched the first four innings. Manager Hall Wells called in Tim Moya as relief pitcher. Four Colts team members made hits. Just two of them, Shane Ranson and Mario Miranda, scored runs.

Underline the subject of each sentence below. Put an **X** next to each sentence that contains a passive verb.

_____ Jacob pitched well.

_____ Some fans were showing poor sportsmanship

_____ The team was coached well.

_____ The opening pitch was thrown by the mayor.

Practice writing sentences with active verbs. First, look at the sentences above that have passive verbs. Rewrite one of those sentences with an active verb. If you need to, add a subject such as *I* or *we* to the sentence.

____

____

Now, write a new paragraph about baseball or another sport. Make sure you use an active verb.

____

____

____

____

____

____

NAME ________________

Lesson 4 The Writing Process: Personal Narrative

Personal narratives can be about ordinary things. They don't have to be about the time you crash-landed an airplane, saved the lives of 17 people, and led everyone over a mountain to safety. If we had to wait for that to happen, almost no one would have anything to write about.

Remember the narrative you read on page 18? Tanner wrote about going to work with his mom. Nothing dangerous or exciting happened. It was just another day, and he learned something along the way. Follow the writing process to develop a personal narrative about one of your own regular days. Maybe you'll learn something along the way.

Prewrite

Look at the idea-starters on page 19 and the notes you made. Choose one of those ideas or another idea that you like, and begin to explore it here.

My idea: ________________

Use this idea web to record details. Write down as many as you can.

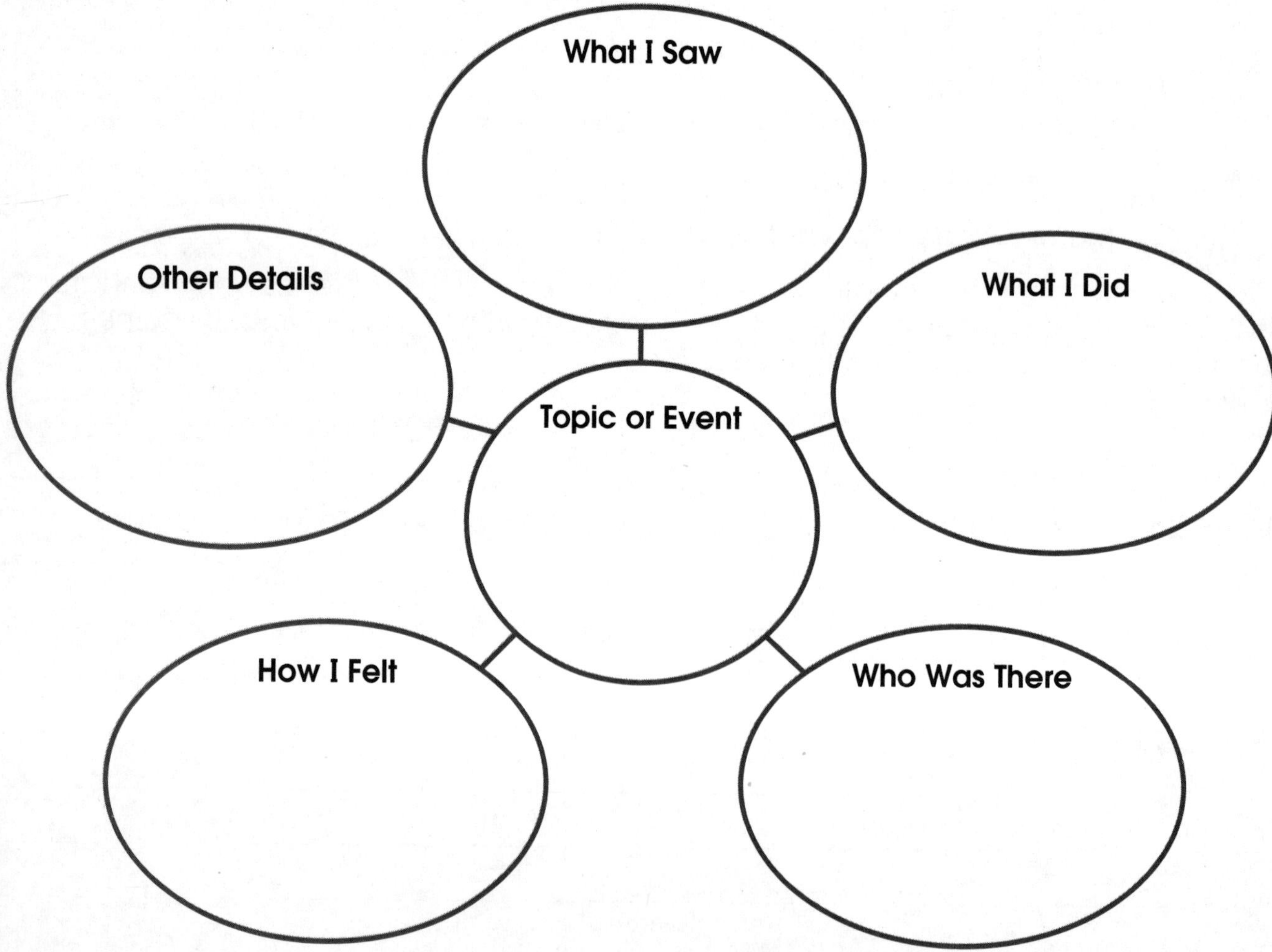

NAME ________________

Lesson 4 The Writing Process: Personal Narrative

So far, you have chosen a topic and recorded ideas. Now, it is time to put your ideas in order. Think about the "story" you are about to tell in your personal narrative. Use the sequence chart on this page to list the events in order. Do not worry about details yet.

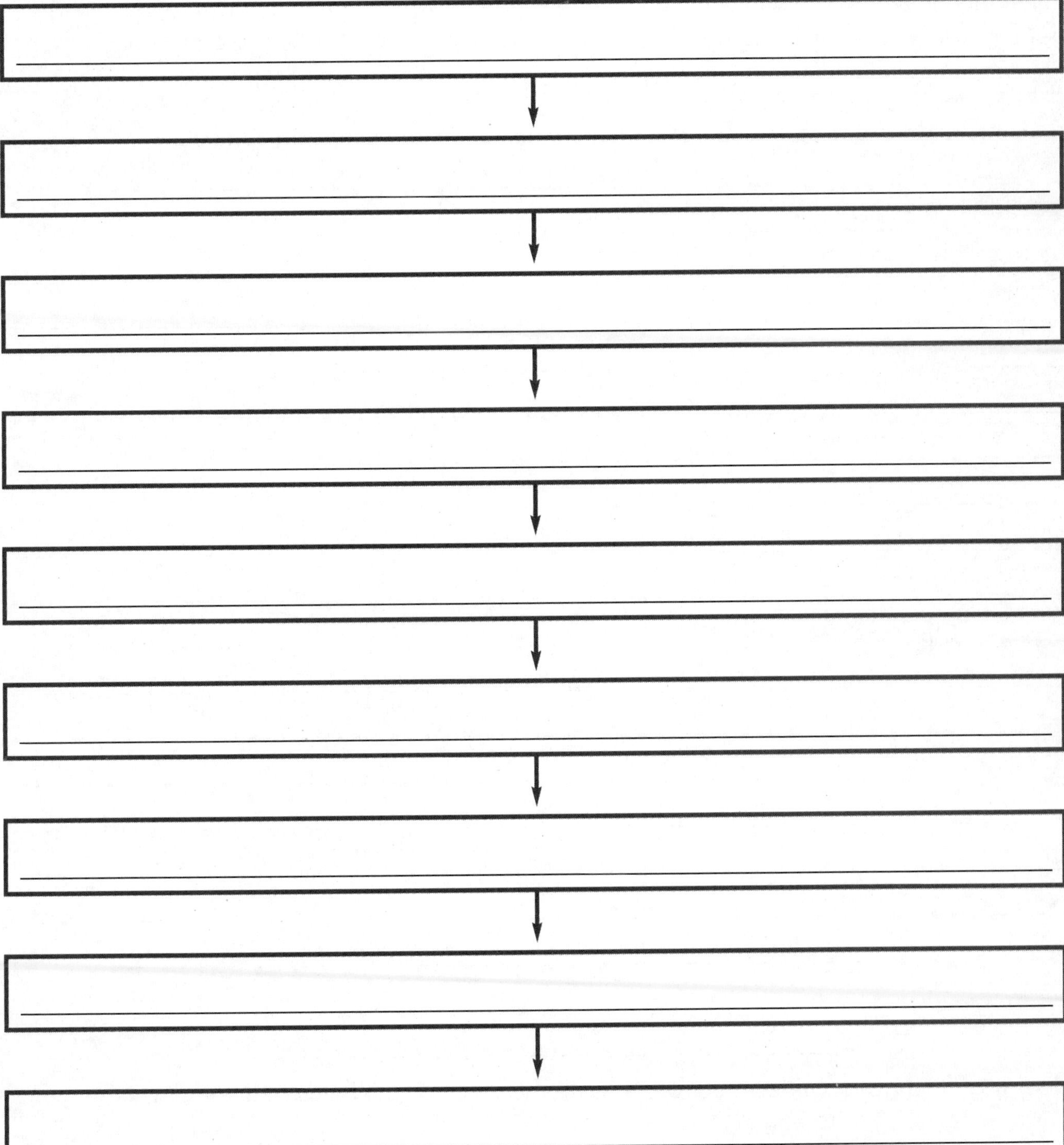

Lesson 4 The Writing Process: Personal Narrative

Draft

Now, write the first draft of your personal narrative. Look back at your sequence chart on page 25 whenever you need to. Write your personal narrative on this page. Continue on another sheet of paper if you need to. As you write, do not worry about getting every word perfect. Just get your ideas down in sentences and in order.

Now that you have written your draft, write an idea for a title here. It is ok if it changes later.

Title: ____________________

NAME ____________________

Lesson 4 The Writing Process: Personal Narrative

Revise

It is hard even for experienced writers to change their work. But every good writer does it. Writers must look closely at a first draft and make sure that it is as good as it can be.

Answer the questions below about your draft. If you answer "no" to any questions, those are the areas that might need improvement. Make notes on your draft about changes you might make later.

- Did you tell about just one "thing" in your narrative?
- Did you include details to make readers feel as if they are right there with you?
- Did you tell events in order? Did you use time and time-order words to show when events happened?
- Did you tell how you felt about the events? Do readers get a sense of your personal feelings?
- Did you use active verbs?
- Does your story flow well when you read it out loud?

Now, focus on making sure you connected with your audience. Did you remember to ask yourself questions such as: Who will read this personal narrative? What might they be interested in? What do they know about me? What might they learn about me from this narrative?

When Tanner wrote his personal narrative about going to work with his mom, he was not sure how to finish it. Finally, he decided his audience would be interested in how he felt about the day. Here is Tanner's final paragraph from page 18.

Spending the day with those people made me realize that ~~those~~ people ^with gray hair aren't just old people. They are funny and full of life and still interested in the world. They made me feel very welcome. ^I wouldn't mind going to work with Mom again some day.

NAME ______________________

Lesson 4 The Writing Process: Personal Narrative

Write the revision of your first draft here. As you revise, remember to keep your audience in mind.

Now that you have revised your draft, are you still happy with your title? If not, write a new title here.

Title: ______________________

Lesson 4 The Writing Process: Personal Narrative

Proofread

Now, correct those last little mistakes. Proofreading is easier if you look for just one kind of error at a time. So, read through once for capital letters. Read again for end punctuation. Read a third time for spelling errors. Here is a checklist to help you proofread your revised narrative.

____ Each sentence begins with a capital letter.

____ Each sentence ends with the correct punctuation (period, question mark, or exclamation point).

____ Each sentence states a complete thought.

____ All words are spelled correctly. (If you're not sure, check a dictionary.)

When proofreaders work, they use certain symbols. Using these symbols makes their job easier. These symbols will make your job easier, too.

- T three little lines under a letter mean that the letter should be capitalized.
- If there is a period missing, do this⊙
- Can you insert a question mark like this?
- Don't ever forget your exclamation points!
- Fix misspelled words like this tis.

Use these symbols as you proofread your personal narrative. Remember to read your writing out loud, even if there is no one to listen. Sometimes, you hear mistakes you do not see.

Publish

Write a final copy of your personal narrative on a separate sheet of paper. Write carefully and neatly so that there are no mistakes.

Chapter 3

NAME ______________________

Lesson 1 Sensory Details

If you were in the midst of this scene, you would learn about everything around you by using all five of your senses: seeing, hearing, smelling, touching, and tasting. When you look at the picture, you have to imagine the sounds, smells, textures, and tastes.

When you write a description, you should also use all five of your senses. How do you use your senses when you write? You use words that help readers use their senses.

Look at the picture again. What do you see? List some things here. Remember to help your readers see things, too. Do you see a stack of trays, or is it a "tower of blue trays"?

What I see: ______________________ ______________________

______________________ ______________________ ______________________

Now, use your other senses and write what you might hear, smell, touch, and taste in this scene.

What I hear: ______________________ ______________________

What I smell: ______________________ ______________________

What I touch: ______________________ ______________________

What I taste: ______________________ ______________________

Lesson 1 Sensory Details

Look back at your lists on page 30. Did you remember to use good sense words so that readers can see, hear, smell, touch, and taste what is in the scene, too? For example, if you wrote that you might hear noises in the kitchen, ask yourself what kind of noises they might be. Is it the *swoosh* of a dishwasher? Is it clanking plates, or the thud of the freezer door? Review your lists and try to add any other words that more clearly describe the sights, sounds, smells, textures, and tastes.

Now, you are going to put your words to work. Describe this scene so clearly that your reader will feel as if he or she is standing right in the middle of it. For this paragraph, organize your ideas by sense. First, describe the sights, then sounds, smells, textures, and tastes. Remember to indent the first sentence of your paragraph.

NAME ______________________

Lesson 2 Adjectives and Adverbs

A sentence needs a noun and a verb. It takes just one of each to make a complete sentence.

Puppies play.

Adjectives and adverbs add description to a sentence.

- An **adjective** is a word that describes a noun or pronoun. Adjectives tell *what kind, how much* or *how many,* and *which ones.* Or, if you prefer to think of it this way, adjectives tell how things look, sound, smell, feel, and taste.
- An **adverb** is a word that describes a verb, an adjective, or another adverb. Adverbs tell *how, when, where,* or *to what degree.* Many adverbs end in **ly**, but some do not.

Adjectives at Work

Starting with a basic sentence, notice how a few adjectives jazz it up.

The puppies rolled and wrestled on the floor.

What kind of puppies are they? *Fuzzy* puppies.

How many puppies are there? *Two* puppies.

What kind of floor is it? A *hard* floor.

Here is the new sentence. Notice that the adjectives go right before the nouns that they describe. This is almost always true. This sentence is much more vivid than the previous one.

Two fuzzy puppies rolled and wrestled on the hard floor.

Now, it is your turn. Look at the sentence below. Think of at least two adjectives to add to it, then write the new sentence. Remember, an adjective tells more about a noun or pronoun.

A child watched the puppies.

____

____

Lesson 2 Adjectives and Adverbs

Adverbs at Work

Start with the same sentence about puppies from page 32 and see how some adverbs liven it up.

The puppies rolled and wrestled on the floor.

When did the puppies roll? *Yesterday.*

How did they wrestle? *Fiercely.*

Here is the new sentence. Notice that one adverb comes several words before the verb it describes. The other falls right after its verb.

Yesterday, the puppies rolled and wrestled fiercely on the floor.

Look at each sentence below. Ask yourself whether you can add information about *how, when, where,* or *to what degree* with an adverb. Write your new sentence on the line.

A child watched the puppies.

____

The dogs went out the door and ran across the yard.

____

Now, look at how both adjectives and adverbs work in this sentence.

old lazily nearly
The ^ dog stretched ^ and ^ fell off the porch.

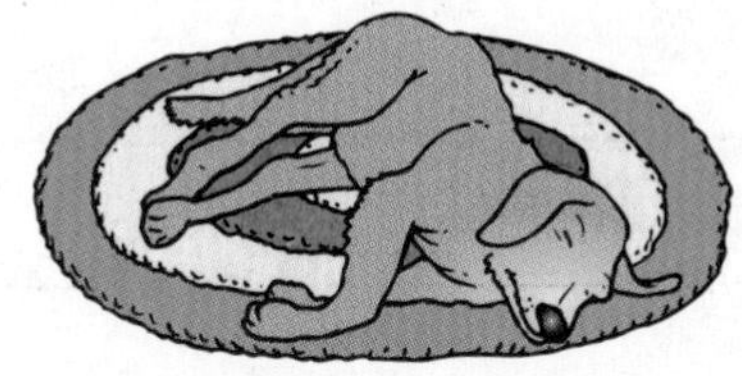

Improve these sentences by adding adjectives and adverbs that make the sentences more vivid.

A pup jumped out of the box.

____

____

A child held a puppy around its tummy.

____

____

NAME ______________________

Lesson 3 Pure Description

When a writer describes an object, readers should be able to see, hear, smell, feel, and perhaps taste it. Can you describe something so vividly that your readers feel as if they are right there seeing it or holding it?

Take a close look at the pen or pencil you have at hand. Look at it as if you are seeing it for the first time. Record details here.

Color: ______________________

Shape: ______________________

Texture: ______________________

Smell: ______________________

Other details: ______________________

Now, write a paragraph in which you describe the pen or pencil. Describe it as if you are not familiar with the object. Remember to appeal to as many of your readers' senses as you can.

NAME ______________________

Lesson 3 Pure Description

Try a more complex object. Look around the room. What object catches your attention? Is it a stapler? A fire extinguisher? A paper clip? Examine it. Even if it is a familiar object, look at it with fresh eyes. Record details of the object here.

Color: ______________________

Shape: ______________________

Texture: ______________________

Smell: ______________________

Other details: ______________________

Now, write a description of the object.

____

____

____

____

____

____

____

____

____

____

____

____

____

On Your Own

It is fun to write descriptions as riddles. For example: What is clear and hard? It has smooth sides and is shaped like a cylinder, but one end is closed. (The answer is *my water glass.*) See if you can lead your friends to name the correct object after hearing your vivid descriptions.

NAME ______________________

Lesson 4 Friendly Letter

A **friendly letter** is a letter written to someone you know. Friendly letters are written to share family news, to cheer someone up, to thank someone for a gift, or just to share or get information. Here is a friendly letter that Erin wrote to her aunt.

There is always a comma after the person's name.

There is a **date** at the top.

This is the **greeting**. The word *Dear* always begins with a capital letter.

March 4

Dear Aunt Rhonda,

How are you doing? I hope it is starting to look like spring down there.

We are studying careers in school. Since you work at the post office, I thought it would be neat to learn about your job. I have several questions:

Do machines really sort the mail?

What rules do you have to know to send and deliver mail?

My teacher also said to ask questions such as what you like and don't like about your job. Could you write back and tell me about your job? I'd really appreciate it!

With love,

Erin

This is the **body** of the letter.

This is the **closing**. The words may be different, but the first word is always capitalized, and there is always a comma after the last word.

The writer always signs his or her name, called a **signature**.

Lesson 4 Friendly Letter

Erin wrote her letter because she wanted some information from her aunt. Most people like to talk about their jobs. Erin has asked some specific questions, which makes it easy for her aunt to respond with the information Erin needs.

Now, write your own friendly letter. Write to someone you know and ask some questions. Maybe you want to know about an uncle's job or about a cousin's school. Look back at the letter on page 36 and follow the format for a friendly letter.

NAME ____________________

Lesson 5 Spatial Organization

When you walk into a room, you normally look around in an organized way. You might scan the room from left to right, or from right to left. If it's a very long, skinny room, you might look from near to far, taking in first what is close and moving on to what is farther away. How you look at a room might depend on the size or shape of the room, what is in the room, or what is happening in the room.

When you describe a room or some other place, you should describe it in an organized way. It is only natural to help your readers "see" the room just as if they were looking at it themselves. In the description of a banquet hall, below, the writer describes the huge room from top to bottom.

Shafts of light shone down from windows high in the wall. The bright beams dazzled my eyes, but did not brighten the room below. The walls, below the windows, were in shadow and nearly invisible. Torches on the walls around the banquet tables burned dimly in comparison with the shafts of sunlight. The tables themselves, made of heavy, darkened wood, did nothing to brighten the room. Only the food looked festive. Spread across the tables were wooden bowls full of bread and platters heaped with steaming meat, potatoes, and vegetables.

When you organize ideas by space, use words that tell where things are. Here are some common spatial words.

above	across	beside	between	beyond	into	left
low	middle	next to	over	right	through	under

Find these, or other spatial words, in the paragraph above. Circle them.

NAME ____________________

Lesson 5 Spatial Organization

Imagine that you are standing at one end of a hallway in your home or school. What do you see? Describe the near end of the hallway first. Then, go on to describe what is part way down the hall, and at the farthest end. Remember to use spatial words to tell where things are.

Now, imagine you are a knight. Your king has sent you to discover everything you can about the castle on page 38. He needs a complete description of the outside of the castle. Write what you can see from your position on the next hill. Decide whether to describe what you can see from side to side (left to right or right to left), from near to far, or from top to bottom.

NAME ______________________________

Lesson 6 Comparisons

A Venn diagram is a tool that helps us compare things.

Ashley is reading *Kira-Kira* by Cynthia Kadohata. She wants to keep track of the two main characters in the book, Lynn and Katie. She makes a Venn diagram to record how the characters are alike and different in the first several chapters of the book.

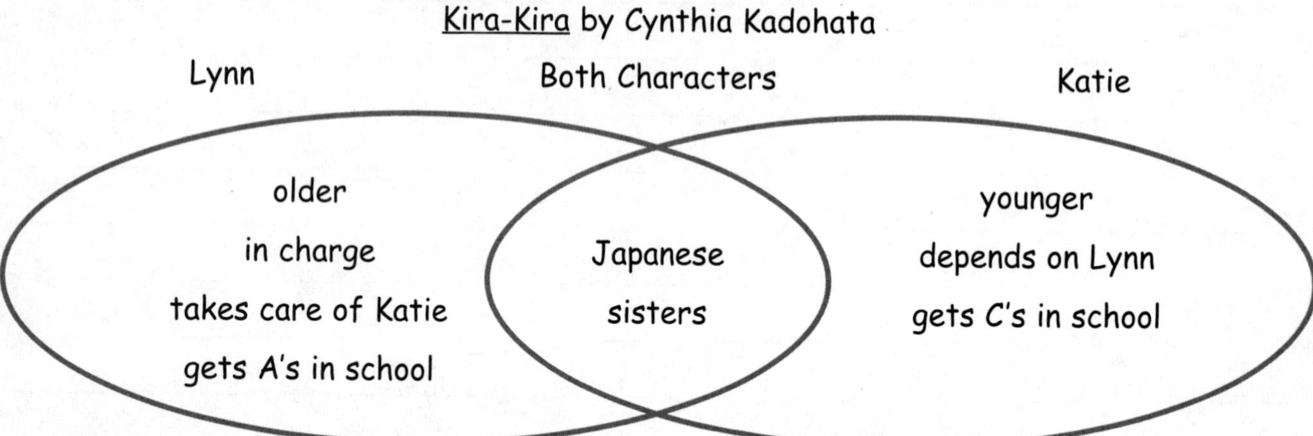

To practice comparing two things, start out with something that you can look at and touch. Get two different textbooks from your desk or from a classroom shelf. Write their titles in the spaces provided. Then, record how each book is different. Finally, write what is the same about both books in the center.

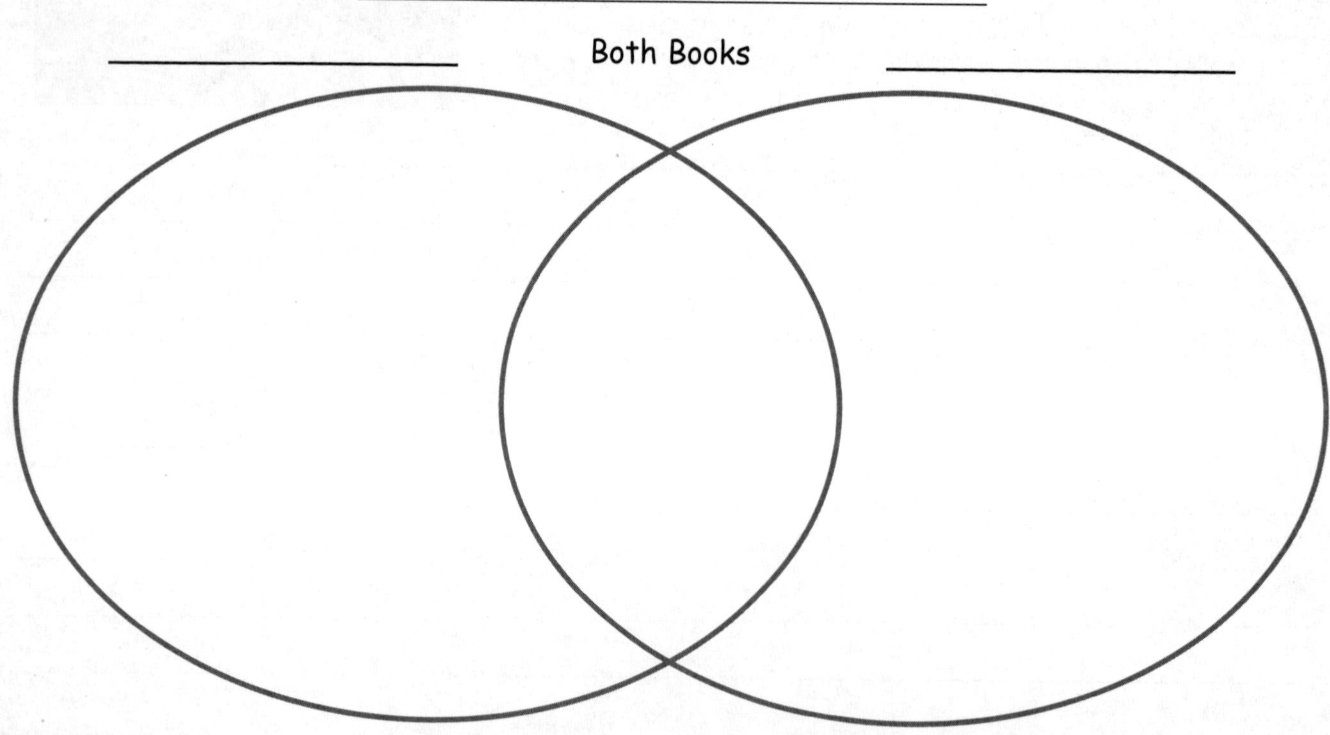

NAME ______________________

Lesson 6 Comparisons

What else would you like to compare? Two different kinds of soap? Computer games? Or, maybe you want to compare two books you have read or two characters from a book, like Ashley did. Choose the items you want to compare and label the circles. Then, write what is the same and different about the items.

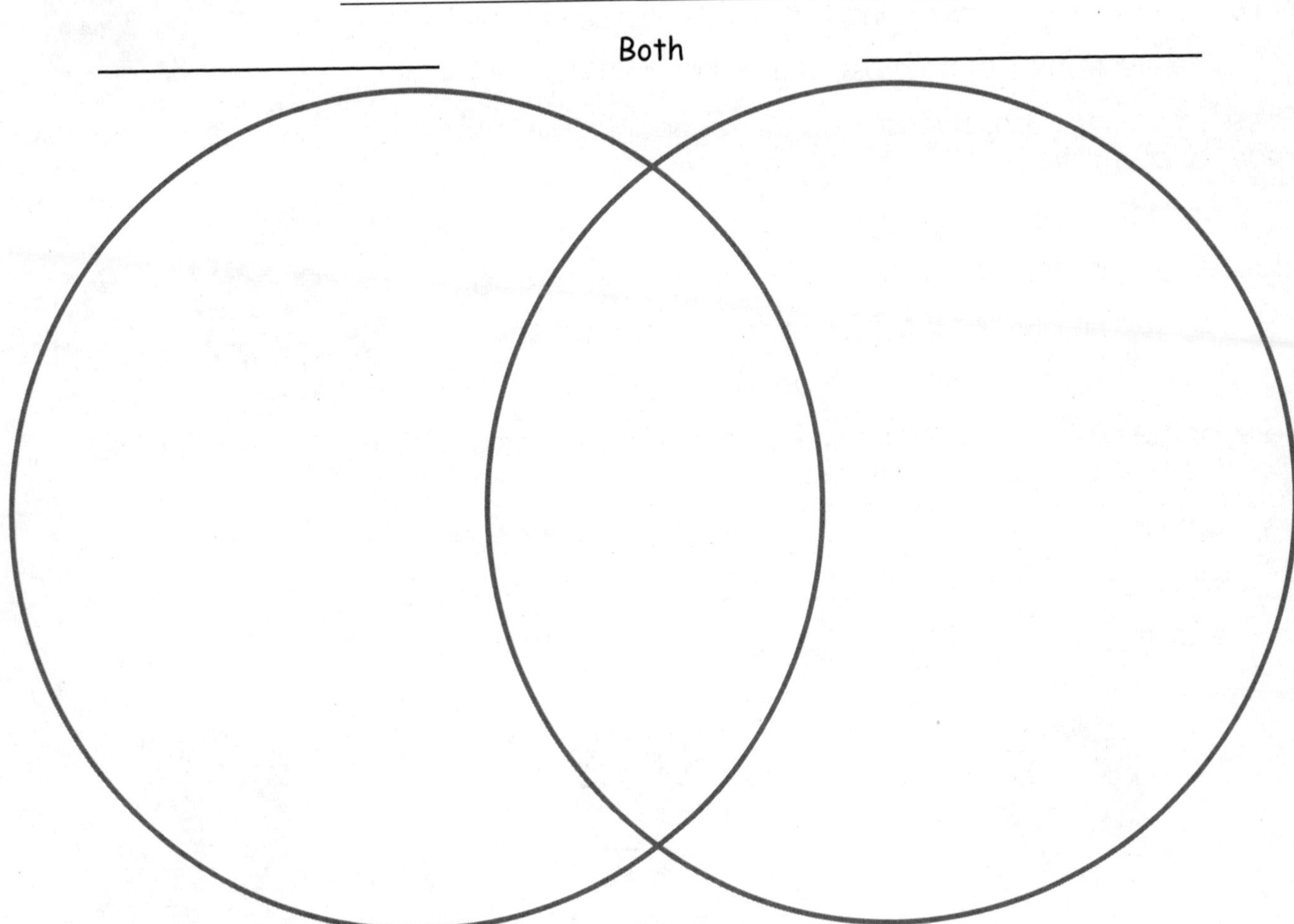

Now, use the information in your diagram to write some sentences.

Write a sentence that tells how the two items are different in some way.

____

____

In a sentence, name one way in which your two items are the same.

____

____

NAME ______________________________

Lesson 7 Compare Two and More Than Two

When you compare two things, the word ending **-er** and the word *more* help you talk and write about how the two things are different.

The first truck is *longer than* the second truck.

Notice how **er** was added to the end of the comparing word *long*.

Now, compare the trucks using the word *massive*.

The first truck is *more massive than* the second truck.

For short words, such as *long*, add an **-er** ending. For longer words, such as *massive*, use *more* to compare.

My apple is *redder than* yours.

Notice that another **d** was added before the **-er** ending.

The red apple also looks *juicier than* the other one.

For *juicy*, change the **y** to **i**, then add **er**.

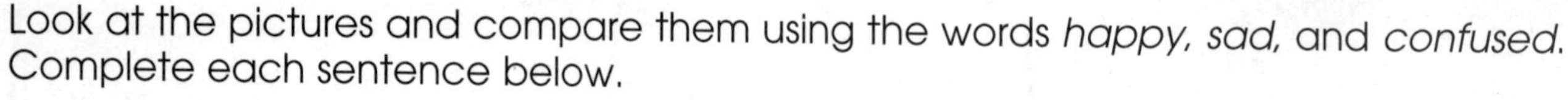

Look at the pictures and compare them using the words *happy, sad,* and *confused.* Complete each sentence below.

Sam is ______________________________ than Alex.

Cal is ______________________________ than Sam.

Alex is ______________________________ than Cal.

NAME ______________________

Lesson 7 Compare Two and More Than Two

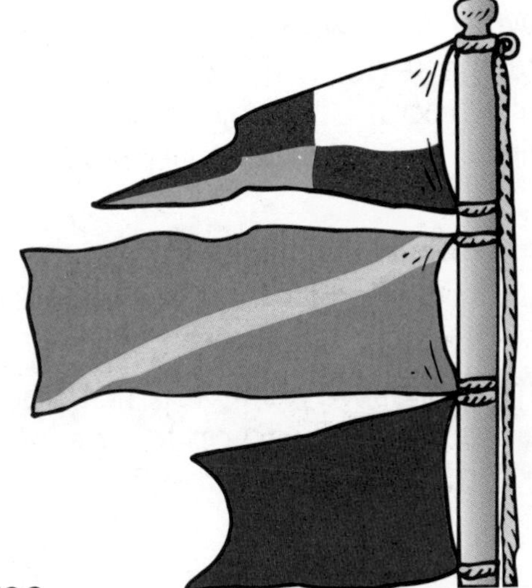

When you talk or write about how three or more things are different, you use the word ending **-est** or the word *most*.

The purple flag is the *lowest* flag.

Sometimes, you have to change the spelling of a word before adding the **-est** ending. Notice the changes made to *big* and *pretty*.

The blue and yellow flag is the *biggest* flag.

The multicolored flag is the *prettiest* flag.

Use *most* instead of adding **-est** with long words.

I think the purple flag is the *most beautiful* of the three.

Look at the picture below. Then, use the words *big, heavy, safe,* and *exciting* in sentences that compare the objects in the pictures. Write one sentence using each word.

____

____

____

____

NAME ___________________________

Lesson 8 Compare Two Objects

When you write to compare, you must present information in a way that makes sense to the reader. There are two ways to organize a written comparison. One way is to talk first about one object, then about the other. Here is an example. Information about the first kitten is in red. Information about the second kitten is in blue.

> I must choose from two kittens. One is black and has a white spot on its chest. It seems very friendly. The other one has gray stripes and is a little fluffier. It seems to be shy.

The other way is to talk first about one feature, or characteristic, as it relates to both objects. Then, go on to another feature, and so on. Here is an example. Again, information about the first kitten is in red. Information about the second kitten is in blue.

> I must choose from two kittens. One is black and has a white spot on its chest. The other has gray stripes and is a little fluffier. The first one seems very friendly. The second one seems shy.

Now, try another comparison between familiar objects. Compare a hippopotamus with a rhinoceros. First, record details about each animal in this Venn diagram.

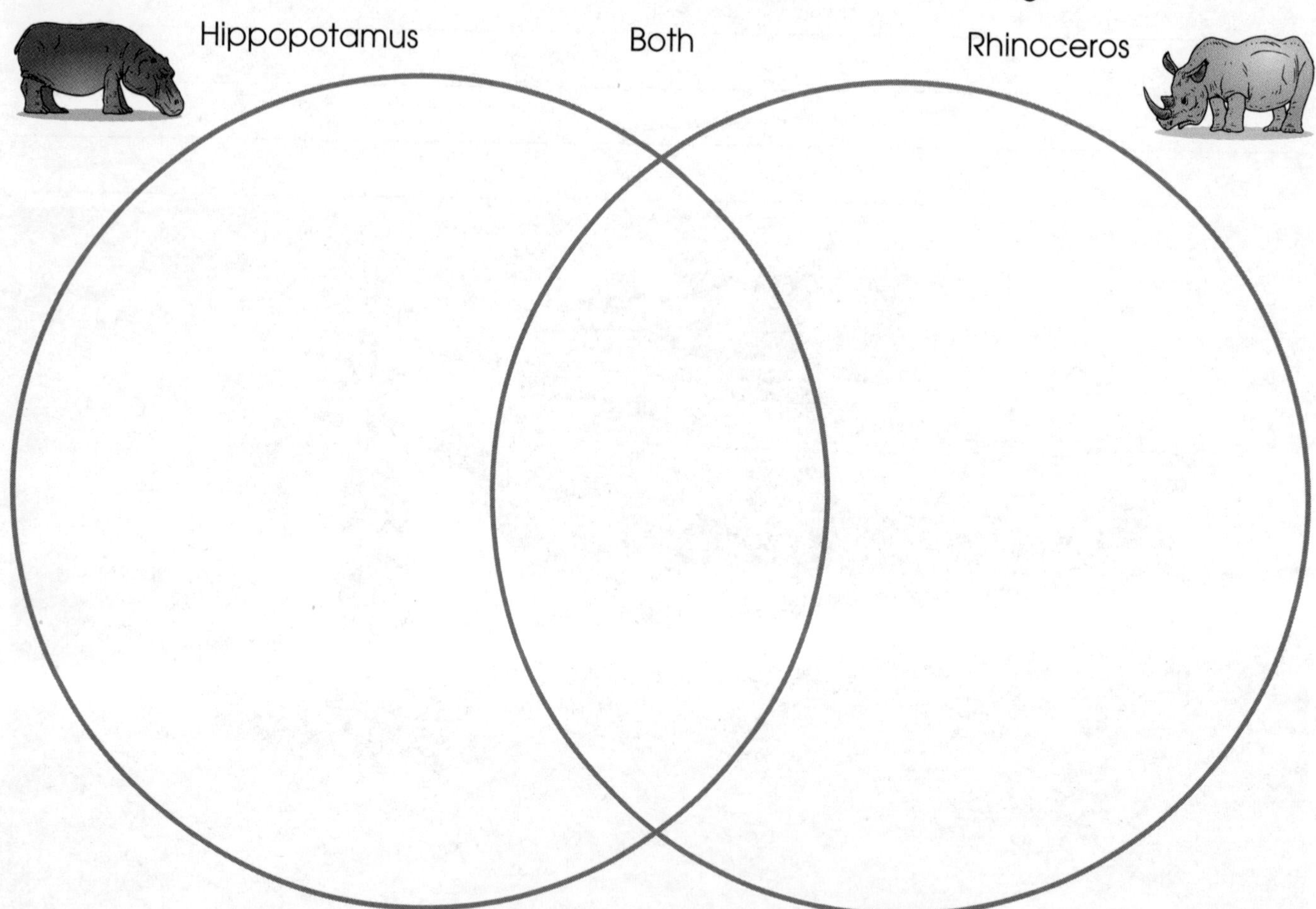

NAME ______________________

Lesson 8 Compare Two Objects

Write a paragraph in which you compare a hippopotamus with a rhinoceros. Write about first one animal then the other.

Now, write another paragraph in which you compare a hippo and a rhino. Now, write about the size of each animal, then about the appearance of each animal, and so on.

NAME ______________________________

Lesson 9 The Writing Process: Descriptive Writing

Whenever you read a story or novel, you are reading descriptive writing. Yes, the author is telling a story with action and dialogue, but he or she is also describing what and where it happens. Whenever writers want to make their readers "see" something, they use descriptive writing. Use the writing process to develop a paragraph that describes the setting of a story.

Prewrite

First, think of some places. They might be real places (a mountain top, a classroom) or made-up places (the far side of Venus or a city deep under the polar icecap). List them here.

Real Places	Made-up Places
______________________	______________________
______________________	______________________
______________________	______________________

Now, look over your lists and think about the places. Which one do you think you can describe most vividly? Choose one and write the place that you decide on here.

Place I will describe: ______________________________

Use this idea web to record details about your place.

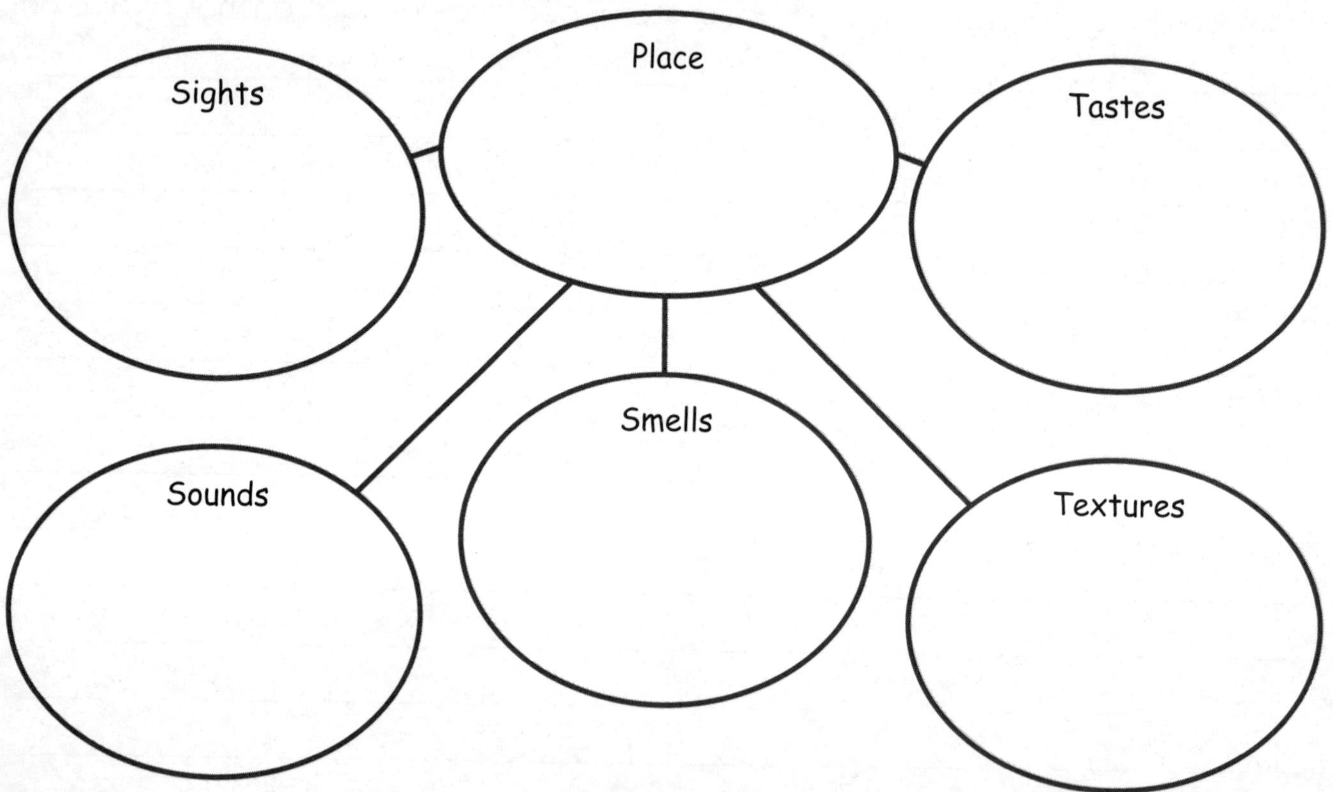

NAME ______________________

Lesson 9 The Writing Process: Descriptive Writing

As a final step in the prewriting stage, organize your ideas. How will you describe this place: from left to right? From top to bottom? Near to far? Make a choice, based on the shape or size of your place.

Method of organization: ______________________

Major details, in order:

Draft

Refer to your prewriting notes as you write a first draft. Remember, this is the time to get your ideas down on paper in sentences. This is not the time to worry about getting every word just right.

____

____

____

____

____

____

____

____

____

____

____

NAME ____________________

Lesson 9 The Writing Process: Descriptive Writing

Revise

All writers face the difficult task of reading what they have just written and trying to make it better. Answer these questions about your draft. If you answer "no" to any of these questions, then those are the areas that might need improvement.

- Did you keep your audience in mind? Did you include details that will interest them and that they will understand?
- Did you organize your description in a logical, spatial way?
- Did you use spatial words to show where things are?
- Did you use vivid verbs and precise nouns to help readers see the place?
- Did you use sense words? To how many of your readers' senses did you appeal?

Rewrite your description here. Make changes to improve your message, based on the questions you just answered.

NAME ______________________

Lesson 9 The Writing Process: Descriptive Writing

Proofread

Your description should be in good shape now. The final task is to check it for any last little errors. It is best to check for one kind of error at a time. Proofread your revision on page 48. Use this checklist to help you catch all of the errors.

____ Does each sentence begin with a capital letter?

____ Does each sentence have an appropriate end mark?

____ Are proper nouns (names of people, places, or things) capitalized?

____ Are all words spelled correctly?

____ Is each paragraph indented?

Publish

Write a final copy of your description here. Use your best printing or handwriting. If you wish, draw a picture of your place on another sheet of paper.

Chapter 4

NAME ______________________

Lesson 1 Parts of a Story

A good story has these ingredients:

- A story tells about made-up people or animals. They are the **characters** in the story.
- A story has a **setting** where the action takes place.
- A story's action is the **plot**. The plot is usually a series of events that includes a problem, or conflict, that needs to be solved.
- A story uses **dialogue**, or conversation among the characters, to move the action of the story along.
- An interesting **beginning**, **middle**, and **end** make a story fun to read.
- **Describing words** tell about the characters, setting, and events.

Read this story. Then, answer the questions on page 52.

City Heat

"Try to think about water," suggested Della.

"What kind of water?" asked her little brother, Dean.

Della shrugged her shoulders, "Any kind. If you think about water, maybe you won't be so hot."

Now, it was Dean's turn to shrug. He usually liked Della's ideas, but he wasn't sure that just thinking about water would cool him off. The August heat bounced off the buildings and sidewalks and made Dean think of an oven. "It's so hot, all I can think of is hot water. Will that work?"

"No, definitely not. You have to think cool, then you'll be cool. Let's go out on the porch and see if it's any better out there." Even on the shady side of the building, there was no relief from the heat. As they settled down to wait for a breath of air, Della gave Dean a suggestion. "Try a cold river flowing down a mountainside."

"Are there fish in the river?" asked Dean.

Della frowned. "Well, I don't know. Does it matter?"

Lesson 1 Parts of a Story

"Well, if I'm going to picture a river, I need to know whether there are fish in it," answered Dean.

"Okay, there are fish in it," said Della.

"What kind?"

"Okay," said Della, impatiently, "this isn't working. Let's go for a walk. Maybe it's cooler down on the ground."

There was even less air down on the sidewalk than there had been on their porch. Talking was too much work, so they just walked. Suddenly, Della said, "Stop right here and close your eyes. Let's try again." Dean obeyed. He was willing to try anything.

"Okay, picture this," Della said. "You are standing at the base of a waterfall. There are no fish because the waterfall is too big and too strong. You can feel the spray on your face..."

"I can feel the spray on my face!" interrupted Dean. He really could feel the spray. New respect for his sister's ideas rose up in him. Then, Della poked his arm. He opened his eyes, and Della was standing there grinning. Beyond her was a fire truck, and past the fire truck was a spouting fire hydrant. Kids and adults were streaming out of the hot brick buildings. A moment later, Della and Dean were right there with them.

NAME ______________________

Lesson 1 Parts of a Story

Answer these questions about "City Heat." Look back at the story if you need to.

Who are the characters in the story?

______________________ ______________________

Where does the action take place?

Setting: ______________________

What words in the story told you where the setting is?

______________ ______________ ______________

What problem occurs?

____

____

____

How does Della solve the problem?

____

____

____

Review the dialogue in the story. Find an example of a line of dialogue that tells you what is happening or what is about to happen.

____

____

____

How does Dean feel about Della? How do you know?

____

____

____

The writer uses words that appeal to readers' senses. Record some of those sense words here. Remember to look for sights, sounds, smells, textures, and tastes.

______________ ______________ ______________

______________ ______________ ______________

Lesson 2 Dialogue

Dialogue is the conversation among characters in a story. Good dialogue helps readers get to know the characters. It also moves the action of the story along. Here is what dialogue looks like.

"Mmm-hmmm?" droned the teller. I took this as my invitation to step up to the window.

"I'd like to make a deposit, please," I said. I had practiced saying it all the way to the bank.

"Mmm-hmmm," she said again.

I slid my envelope across the smooth counter. I felt the need to explain, so I added, "It's everything I saved."

"Mmm-hmmm."

"It's my recycling money," I went on. "I've been picking up aluminum cans all summer."

"Mmm-hmmm," she said. I wondered how she could count money and listen to me all at the same time.

What do you learn about the teller from this dialogue?

___

What do you learn about the narrator (the other speaker)?

___

Take a closer look at a line of dialogue and its punctuation.

The **tag line** tells who is speaking.

Quotation marks go before and after the speaker's exact words.

I felt the need to explain, so I added, "It's everything I saved."

A **comma** separates the speaker's words from the tag line.

The first word that a speaker says begins with a capital letter, even if that word is not the first word of the entire sentence.

NAME ____________________

Lesson 2 Dialogue

Below is some dialogue that has not been punctuated. Add the punctuation. Look at the story on page 53 for examples if you need to.

Here is your deposit slip said the teller.

I took it and said Thank you, ma'am.

Do you need anything else she asked.

Dialogue should sound like real people talking. A ten-year-old character should sound like a kid. An adult should sound like a grown-up. Remember that adults sound different from each other. The president of a bank would sound much different from the bored bank teller, like the one in the dialogue on page 53.

Write a conversation between yourself and a bank president. Make the dialogue sound realistic. Stop and think how you would speak to a business person sitting behind a large desk. Remember to use quotation marks and tag lines. Look at the examples on page 53 if you need to. The first line of dialogue has been done for you.

"I would like to deposit a large amount of money in your bank, please."

NAME ____________________

Lesson 3 Setting

You're watching a scary movie. That low, rumbling music is rising again, and you just know something bad is going to happen. Movie directors use music to help set the tone, or mood, of a movie. When you write, you have to rely on the setting to help set the tone. The setting of a story is when and where the story's action takes place.

In some stories, readers learn some details of the setting almost by accident. Perhaps the narrator looks out a window and comments on "the bustling city" below. Maybe a character is a passenger in a covered wagon, so readers know that the story is set in the mid- to late 1800s.

In other stories, the narrator describes the setting. Here is an example from F. Scott Fitzgerald's short story, "Winter Dreams."

> In the fall when the days became crisp and gray, and the long Minnesota winter shut down like the white lid of a box, Dexter's skis moved over the snow that hid the fairways of the golf course.

Look at all the information in that one sentence:

It is early winter.

Someone is in Minnesota.

A character's name is Dexter.

He skis, and he is skiing across a golf course.

Besides information, there is also a mood. It is a quiet, reflective mood.

What can you do in one sentence? Use Fitzgerald's sentence above as a model. Write about something that happens during a certain season. Name the season at the beginning of the sentence like Fitzgerald did. Remember to use commas and transition words to keep your sentence complete and clear.

NAME ______________________________

Lesson 3 Setting

Here is another example of a setting described by a narrator. This passage is from "The Hound of the Baskervilles" by Arthur Conan Doyle.

> Now and then we passed a moorland cottage, walled and roofed with stone, with no creeper to break its harsh outline. Suddenly we looked down into a cuplike depression, patched with stunted oaks and firs which had been twisted and bent by the fury of years of storm. Two high, narrow towers rose over the trees. The driver pointed with his whip.
>
> "Baskerville Hall," said he.

What information do you get about the setting from this passage?

____

____

____

____

What mood, or feeling, do you get from the passage?

____

____

____

Writers use details in their settings that match the mood of what is happening in the story. First, think about details that a writer might include in a very happy part of a story.

What might the weather be like?

____

What time of day might it be?

____

In what kinds of places might the characters be?

__________ __________ __________

NAME ______________________

Lesson 3 Setting

Now, think about setting details that a writer might include in a scary part of a story.

What might the weather be like?

____

What time of day might it be?

____

In what kinds of places might the characters be?

______________ ______________ ______________

Look back over the details you recorded for happy settings and scary settings. Are you starting to imagine a great story? Choose one of the settings you have already begun to visualize and develop it further here.

Write a paragraph that describes the setting. Indicate both when and where the action takes place. Remember to organize your details in a way that makes sense.

____

____

____

____

____

____

____

____

____

____

____

____

____

NAME ______________________________

Lesson 4 Characters

Think of a character from a book you have read. Do you remember feeling good when the character felt good and bad when the character felt bad? Name some of your favorite characters.

______________________________ ______________________________

______________________________ ______________________________

Now, think about what you know about those characters. How did you learn about them? How did the narrator or author help you get to know the character? Normally, readers learn about characters in four ways. You learn from:

- what the narrator tells you.
- what the character says and how he or she says it.
- what the character does.
- what other characters say about the character.

Look at your list of characters above. Choose one that you really liked or remember well. Write what you know about that character. For each detail you record, write how you know it. For example, you might know that a character is bold because she stood up in front of the class on her first day in a new school and told her whole life story. You might know that a character is adopted because another character reveals that information in dialogue.

Character: ______________________________

What I Know About the Character	How I Know It
______________________________	______________________________
______________________________	______________________________
______________________________	______________________________

NAME ______________________

Lesson 4 Characters

Now, think about a character you would like to create. Rather than thinking about what happens to the character, think about what kind of person the character is. Answer these questions.

Is the character human? ______ If not, what is the character? ____________________

Is the character male or female? ________________

What two words best describe your character?

____________________________________ ____________________________________

What background details or family history might be important to readers?

____

What might your character say, and how? Write a line of dialogue that your character might speak.

____

What might other characters say about this character? Either show some dialogue or describe what others would say.

____

Now, introduce your character. Write a paragraph about him or her.

____

____

____

____

____

____

____

____

____

____

NAME ______________________

Lesson 5 Point of View

When a writer writes a story, he or she chooses a narrator to tell the story. In some stories, the narrator is one of the characters in the story. Words such as *I, me,* and *my* let readers know that this is happening. This is called **first-person point of view**. Here is a piece of a story written in first person.

"Hey, kid. Give me your lunch." That was all that Larry Garvin ever said to me. I had come to think of him simply as L.G., short for Lunch Grabber.

"Why do you let him do that?" my friend Rico asked after watching yet another lunch grab.

I gave him one of those "duh" looks. "He's twice my size, Rico! Besides, when he doesn't take my lunch, he doesn't have anything to eat. Mom has started packing two lunches." Rico's eyes popped as I pulled a second lunch out of my backpack.

Here is the same scene, but it is written in **third-person point of view**. The narrator "reports" all the action, but does not take part in it. In this case, the narrator is all-knowing. In other words, the narrator knows the thoughts and feelings of all the characters. Readers see words such as *he, she, him, her, his, they,* and *them* in stories that are written in third person.

"Hey, kid. Give me your lunch." That was all that Larry Garvin ever said to James. James had come to think of Larry simply as "L.G.," short for Lunch Grabber.

"Why do you let him do that?" James's friend Rico asked after watching yet another lunch grab.

James gave him one of those "duh" looks. "He's twice my size, Rico! Besides, when he doesn't take my lunch, he doesn't have anything to eat. Mom has started packing two lunches." Rico's eyes popped as James pulled a second lunch out of his backpack.

NAME ____________________

Lesson 5 Point of View

Look back at the piece of the story on page 60. What do you think the bully, Larry Garvin, was thinking? Write another version of this scene from the first-person point of view, with Larry as the narrator. Here is the first line. You can take it from there.

"Hey, kid. Give me your lunch," I said.

Now, practice writing in third-person point of view. The next day, instead of allowing Larry to take his lunch, James simply offers it to him. How does Larry respond? Write this scene in third person with an all-knowing narrator. You may choose to reveal the inner thoughts and feelings of James, Larry, Rico, or all three.

NAME ______________________________

Lesson 6 Stories Are Everywhere

Many stories that you read are **realistic**. They include human characters who are more or less normal people. They live on Earth, whether in the past or present. Though their characters come from a writer's imagination, they could be real, and the events could actually happen.

List some stories or books you have read that are realistic.

______________________________ ______________________________

______________________________ ______________________________

______________________________ ______________________________

What kind of realistic story would you like to write? Will it be about an adventure that a kid had on the frontier in 1870 or a modern-day kid who is trying to break the all-time swimming record at his school? Jot down some realistic story ideas here.

Realistic story idea #1

Character(s): ______________________________

Setting: (time) ______________________________

(place) ______________________________

Plot: ______________________________

____

____

Realistic idea #2

Character(s): ______________________________

Setting: (time) ______________________________

(place) ______________________________

Plot: ______________________________

____

____

NAME ____________________

Lesson 6 Stories Are Everywhere

Do you remember Paul Bunyan and Pecos Bill? They are characters from **tall tales**. It is easy to remember them because their stories include such outrageous details. The writers of these tales use exaggeration; they stretch details to make them funny or perhaps just strange. Tall tale characters could not be real, and the events could not actually happen.

Think of tall tales you have read. Try to recall some of the exaggerated details. For example, how big was the character? How did he or she travel? Those are the kinds of details that are fun to exaggerate.

What kind of tall tale would you like to write? Who will be your main characters? Where will they live and what will they do? Let your imagination go and write down a couple of tall tale ideas here.

Tall tale idea #1

Character(s): ____________________

Setting: (time) ____________________

(place) ____________________

Plot: ____________________

____

____

Details to exaggerate: ____________________

Tall tale idea #2

Character(s): ____________________

Setting: (time) ____________________

(place) ____________________

Plot: ____________________

____

____

Details to exaggerate: ____________________

NAME ____________________

Lesson 7 The Writing Process: Story

Some story writers like to use settings and situations they have experienced themselves. Others like to go beyond themselves and use exaggeration to create funny, often wild, worlds. Use the writing process and see what kind of world you can create.

Prewrite

Look again at the story ideas you wrote on pages 62 and 63. Choose one of those ideas, or another idea that you like, and begin to develop it. Whether you are writing a realistic story or a tall tale, you will need to pay special attention to your main character. Use this idea web to record details about how he or she looks, acts, speaks, and so on.

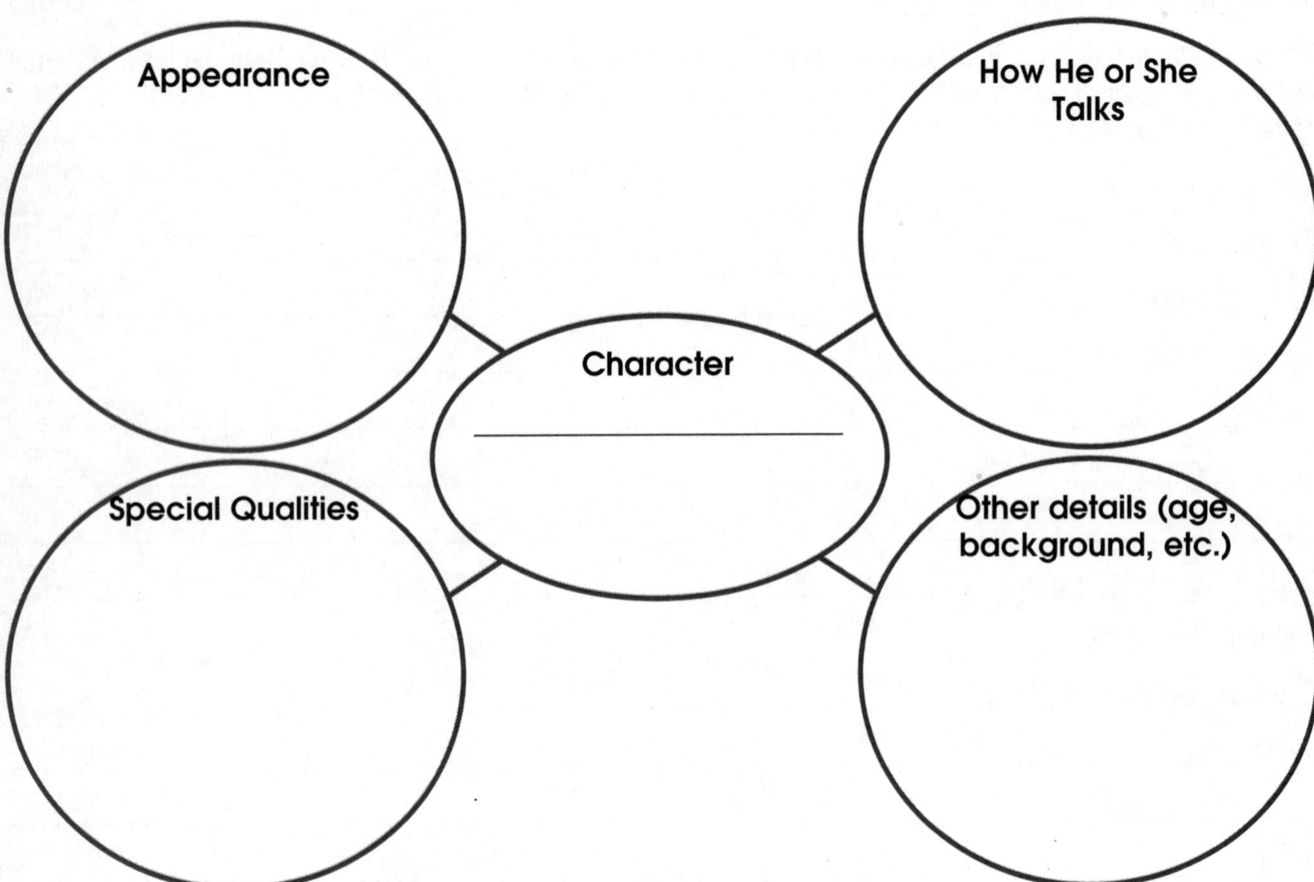

Before you continue, consider these questions about your setting and plot.

- What is the setting of your story? Consider place or location, season, time of day, weather conditions, and so on.
- What is the character's problem?
- What does the character do to try to solve the problem? Does it take more than one try? What is the final solution or outcome?

NAME ______________________

Lesson 7 The Writing Process: Story

Now, it is time to put the parts of your story together. Think about the story you are about to tell. Use the story map on this page to list the important parts of your story.

Character(s)

____

Setting

____

Plot: Beginning

____

____

____

____

____

Plot: Middle

____

____

____

____

____

Plot: End

____

____

____

____

____

NAME ____________________

Lesson 7 The Writing Process: Story

Draft

Write a first draft of your story. Refer to your story map as you write your story on this page. Continue on another sheet of paper if you need to. As you write, do not worry about making mistakes. Just get your ideas down in sentences and in order.

Now that you have written your draft, write an idea for a title here. It might change later, but that's okay.

Title: ____________________

NAME ____________________

Lesson 7 The Writing Process: Story

Revise

Every writer must look at his or her work with fresh eyes and figure out how to make the writing better. Even experienced writers do this, and no one considers it an easy job.

Answer the questions below. If you answer "no" to any of these questions, those are the areas you might need to improve. Write notes on your draft so you know what needs attention.

- Did you give details about an interesting character and a setting?
- Did you include a problem and a solution in your plot?
- Did you tell events in an order that made sense?
- Did you create pictures in your readers' minds with vivid adjectives and adverbs?
- If you wrote a tall tale, did you stretch details to make them funny?
- Did you use dialogue to help readers learn about characters and to move the story forward?
- Did you describe how things look, sound, smell, feel, and taste?

Now, review the important parts of a story.

- In the beginning of a story, readers meet the characters and learn a little about the setting and the plot. The first sentence of a story should make readers want to keep on reading.
- In the middle of a story, the action takes place. Readers see the character or characters face a problem. The characters probably make one or more attempts to solve the problem.
- In the end, the characters solve the problem in a logical way. Remember, it is not satisfying to read a story in which a big problem just goes away by magic.

On your draft, draw brackets around the beginning, middle, and end of your story. Write some notes if you decide that you must change any of those parts to make them more interesting for your readers.

NAME ______________________________

Lesson 7 The Writing Process: Story

Write the revision of your first draft here. As you revise, remember to look for vivid details that appeal strongly to your readers' senses.

Now that you have revised your draft, are you still happy with your title? If not, now is your chance to change it.

Title: ______________________________

NAME ____________________

Lesson 7 The Writing Process: Story

Proofread

Now, correct those last little mistakes. Proofreading is easier if you look for just one kind of error at a time. So, read through once for capital letters. Read again for end punctuation. Read a third time for spelling errors. Here is a checklist to help you proofread your revised story.

____ Each sentence begins with a capital letter.

____ Each sentence ends with the correct punctuation (period, question mark, or exclamation point).

____ Dialogue is punctuated correctly.

____ Each sentence states a complete thought.

____ All words are spelled correctly.

When proofreaders work, they use certain symbols. Using these symbols makes their job easier. These symbols will make your job easier, too.

- T three little lines under a letter mean that the letter should be capitalized.
- Write in missing end marks like this: ⊙ ? !
- "Please add a comma and quotation marks," she said.
- Fix incorrect or misspelled words like ~~these~~ this.

Use these symbols as you proofread your story. Remember to read your writing out loud, even if there is no one to listen. When you read out loud, you may hear mistakes or rough spots that you did not see.

Publish

If you wish, write a final copy of your story on a separate sheet of paper. Write carefully and neatly so that there are no mistakes. Then, add illustrations and make a neat cover or title page. Share your story with friends and family.

Chapter 5

NAME ____________________

Lesson 1 Persuasive Writing

Advertisements are one form of persuasive writing. Letters to the editor are another. A written speech may be persuasive. An article or essay can also be persuasive. For example, a scientist might write an article or essay to persuade other scientists that a theory is correct. A politician might write an article to persuade voters to support a local issue. Whatever the form that persuasive writing takes, the writer's goal is to try to make readers think, feel, or act in a certain way.

Here is an example of a short persuasive article.

Recess Before Lunch Is the Best Bet

By Pamela Whitaker
Principal, Tri-City Elementary School

For decades, elementary schools have followed a routine that puts lunch before recess. Recently, however, a few schools have broken the mold and switched to recess before lunch. Tri-City Elementary is one of those schools.

At recess, students burn off energy and build up appetites. Then, they come into the lunchroom really ready to eat. They drink more because they have just been exercising. According to the school nurse, taking in extra liquids helps children feel better and stay healthier. Students discard less food because their appetites are better, and they are not hurrying to be first out to the playground. Finally, the teachers believe that students return to the classroom more ready to learn.

Teachers, staff, parents, and students all think the new system is great. I would encourage every elementary school in the country to schedule recess before lunch.

NAME ____________________

Lesson 1 Persuasive Writing

Do you think recess before lunch is a good idea, or do you prefer lunch before recess? Respond to Ms. Whitaker's article on page 70. State your opinion and support it with reasons. Pretend that your article will appear in the school newspaper and give it a title. Make sure that your opinion is clear and that readers understand what you want them to think or do. See how persuasive you can be.

____

by ____________________

NAME ______________________

Lesson 2 Facts and Opinions

Which of the following sentences is a fact? Which is an opinion? If you are not sure, ask yourself these questions: Which statement could be proven true? That would be a **fact**. Which is a belief or a personal judgment? That would be an **opinion**.

Our school cafeteria serves lunch to 448 children each day.

Our school cafeteria serves the best food in the school district.

Often, writers state both facts and opinions. That is okay, but readers must be sure to distinguish between the two. Look for facts and opinions as you read Ms. Whitaker's article again.

Recess Before Lunch Is the Best Bet

By Pamela Whitaker
Principal, Tri-City Elementary School

For decades, elementary schools have followed a routine that puts lunch before recess. Recently, however, a few schools have broken the mold and switched to recess before lunch. Tri-City Elementary is one of those schools.

At recess, students burn off energy and build up appetites. Then, they come into the lunchroom really ready to eat. They drink more because they have just been exercising. According to the school nurse, taking in extra liquids helps children feel better and stay healthier. Students discard less food because their appetites are better, and they are not hurrying to be first out to the playground. Finally, the teachers believe that students return to the classroom more ready to learn.

Teachers, staff, parents, and students all think the new system is great. I would encourage every elementary school in the country to schedule recess before lunch.

NAME ______________________

Lesson 2 Facts and Opinions

Words such as *think, believe, should, must, never, always, like, hate, best,* and *worst* may signal that a statement is an opinion. Scan the article on page 72 again and circle any opinion signal words you find,

Write two facts from the article.

____

____

Write two opinions from the article.

____

____

Akira, a student at Tri-City Elementary, has written about the new lunch routine. Read the paragraph he wrote.

> I used to eat my lunch in about 6 minutes. Terry and I used to race to see who could finish first. Recess is much more fun than lunch. Now that we have recess first, I don't eat so fast. Mom thinks I must be growing because I eat such big lunches now. I think recess is still more fun than lunch, but lunch is okay, too.

Write one fact from Akira's paragraph.

____

____

Circle any opinion signal words that you find in Akira's paragraph. Then, write one opinion that Akira states.

____

____

Now, based on Ms. Whitaker's and Akira's facts, state your own opinion about having recess before lunch.

____

____

NAME ______________________

Lesson 3 Emotional Appeals

How do writers get readers to think, feel, or act in a certain way when they write persuasively? They often appeal to readers' emotions. When writers make an **emotional appeal**, they try to get at something about which readers feel strongly. For example, Devon thinks that teachers shouldn't assign homework on weekends. He included this statement in a letter to the editor of the school paper:

> We work hard at school during the week, but the weekend should be our time to relax and play with friends. I don't think it is fair that teachers give us homework over the weekend. We already spend all of our free time doing homework on weeknights.

Devon knows that most students feel strongly about homework. He also knows that students like to have time to play with friends. Though the statements are opinions (rather than facts), they have a strong emotional appeal and may persuade some readers to believe as the writer does.

Many people have strong feelings about positive issues such as these:

home	family	comfort	money
safety	justice	conservation	security

People may also have strong feelings toward negative issues such as these:

crime	injustice	waste
pollution	violence	danger

Name some issues about which you have strong feelings.

______________ ______________ ______________

______________ ______________ ______________

______________ ______________ ______________

Emotional appeals may tie into readers' positive or negative feelings. Read the letter to the editor on the next page. It makes an emotional appeal to a negative issue.

NAME ____________________

Lesson 3 Emotional Appeals

Dear Editor:

I am writing to voice my opinion on weekend homework. Kids our age need to spend more time exercising and playing with friends, not stuck inside working on homework. We work hard all week, writing book reports and doing math problems. By the end of the week, our brains are full and need to rest. We would learn even more if we didn't have to do homework over the weekend.

Devon

Ms. Tierney's 5th-grade class

Explain the emotional appeal in Devon's letter to the editor.

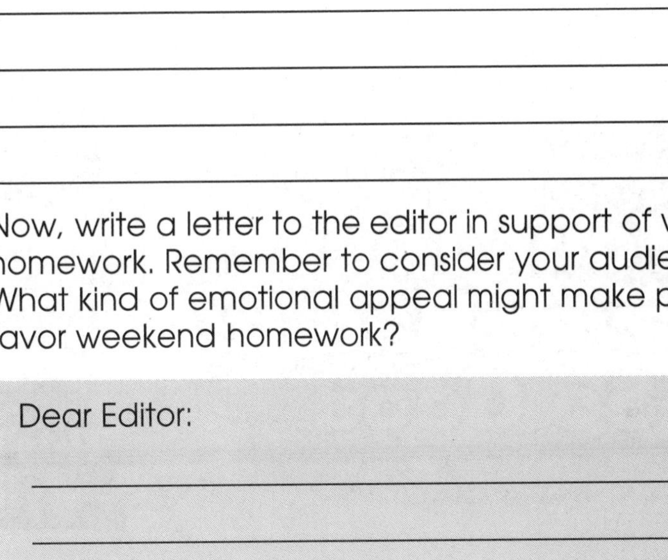

____

____

____

____

Now, write a letter to the editor in support of weekend homework. Remember to consider your audience. What kind of emotional appeal might make people favor weekend homework?

Dear Editor:

NAME ______________________

Lesson 4 Advertising

People who write advertisements are persuasive writers. They rely heavily on emotional appeals to convince the reader to buy their product. They know that people have strong feelings about wanting to feel good, to fit in, and to have fun. Advertisements constantly send people the messages people want to hear.

What message does the sock slogan send? (In other words, to what strong emotion does it appeal?)

____

____

What message does the eyeglass slogan send?

____

____

You already know that writers need to consider their audience when they write. Advertising writers know that thinking about their audience is especially important. Perhaps the most often-asked question is this: Who might buy this product, and what will persuade them to do so?

Suppose you are writing an advertisement for baby clothing. Who is your audience?

____

____

To what strong feelings do you need to appeal to get your audience to buy your baby clothing?

____

____

NAME ______________________________

Lesson 4 Advertising

Would you make a good advertising copywriter? Create a slogan for a barbershop or a beauty salon. First, think about who the audience is. About what kinds of issues might they have strong feelings? In your slogan, make an emotional appeal.

Now, your next assignment is to create a slogan for a used car lot. Again, think of your audience and make an emotional appeal.

Create a new slogan for your school. Consider the strong feelings people have about keeping children safe, educating them, and feeling pride for both school and community.

Images can make emotional appeals, as well, and most advertisements use a combination of words and images to persuade people to buy a product. Look back at the slogans you created. Choose your favorite and create an image to accompany it. Your slogan and image should work together to make a very strong emotional appeal. Create your ad below.

NAME ______________________________

Lesson 5 Order of Importance

When writers write about events, they use time order. When they describe a place, they use spatial order. When they write to persuade, they use **order of importance**.

Remember, when writers write to persuade, they try to make their readers think or act in a certain way. For example, you might try to persuade community members to donate canned food to the student council's food drive. As you persuade, you should save your most important ideas—your strongest arguments—for last. So, build ideas from least important to most important.

Student Council Food Drive

The Student Council's fall project is a food drive. The class that collects the most cans will earn book fair coupons. All canned goods collected will go to the Fourth Street Food Pantry. The Fourth Street Food Pantry provides food to approximately 60 families each week during the summer. In the winter, that number nearly doubles as winter heating bills rise and families have less money to spend on food. These families rely on the Food Pantry to keep themselves fed and healthy. If we all help just a little bit, keeping the Food Pantry stocked will be easy.

This writer gave several reasons why people should donate to the food drive. Can you find them? Number them in the paragraph. Then, underline the most important reason.

NAME ______________________

Lesson 5 Order of Importance

What charity project do you think your student council could do? Maybe you could raise money to save the rainforest. Choose an issue you feel strongly about. Then, write a letter to your teacher or principal. Try to persuade the person that your idea is a good one. Ask yourself this: What will make this person want to support my issue?

Before you begin drafting your letter, write your reasons here. Then, number them in the order in which you will use them in your letter. Save the strongest argument or most important reason for last.

Reason: ______________________

Reason: ______________________

Reason: ______________________

Reason: ______________________

Dear ______________________,

Lesson 6 Business Letter

A **business letter** is a letter written to a company, organization, or person you do not know. Writers usually write business letters to make a request, to express a concern, or to make a complaint. Whatever the reason for writing the letter, the writer usually wants the recipient to do something, so there may be an element of persuasion. It is important to be very clear about the action the recipient should take. Read this business letter, which is a letter of request. Notice its six parts.

The **heading** includes the sender's address and the date.

1829 Marshall Avenue
Erie, PA 16509
October 12, 2008

The **inside address** is the name and address of the recipient.

Fourth Street Food Pantry
827 N. Fourth Street
Erie, PA 16509

A colon follows the **greeting**.

Dear Fourth Street Food Pantry:

The text of the letter is the **body**.

I am a member of the student council at Weber Elementary. For our fall project, we are having a food drive. We will donate everything we collect to the Food Pantry. Before we begin, I have some questions. We want to make sure that we collect the kinds of foods you need.

Should we collect only canned foods, or are "dry" items such as breakfast cereals and soup mixes okay as well? Please contact our advisor, Mrs. Burton, during the day at 555-2112 with this information.

A comma follows the **closing**.

Thank you,

The sender always includes a **signature**.

Miriam Medina

Miriam Medina

Lesson 6 Business Letter

Weeks have passed and the food drive has gone very well. There is so much canned food stacked up in the gym that you need a truck to get it to the food pantry. Write to Mr. Strouse, the father of one of your classmates, who owns a delivery truck company. Ask that he donate his time to load and deliver the collected canned goods to the pantry. Remember, you must think about how to get him to want to do this for you. Be polite and persuasive. Also, be clear about how and when he should respond to your request.

1829 Marshall Avenue
Erie, PA 16509
December 18, 2008

Mr. Milt Strouse
Strouse Trucking
11674 Granger Road
Erie, PA 16509

NAME ______________________

Lesson 7 The Writing Process: Persuasive Article

The teachers and staff at your school work hard to make the school a good one. They want to make it even better, so they have asked how you think the school could be improved. Use the writing process to create a persuasive article about a change that you think would improve your school.

Prewrite

Write notes here about some things that could be improved at your school.

What Could Be Improved	How It Could Be Improved
______________________	______________________
______________________	______________________
______________________	______________________

Now, think about these issues for a few minutes. Which one do you feel most strongly about? Which change do you think is the most important? Write your choice here.

____

Use this idea web to record your reasons for suggesting this change. Remember, your goal is to persuade the teachers and staff that the change you are suggesting would be a good one for the school. What will make them agree with you? In addition to stating your opinion, you will have to give good reasons for believing as you do. Add more ovals to the idea web if you need to.

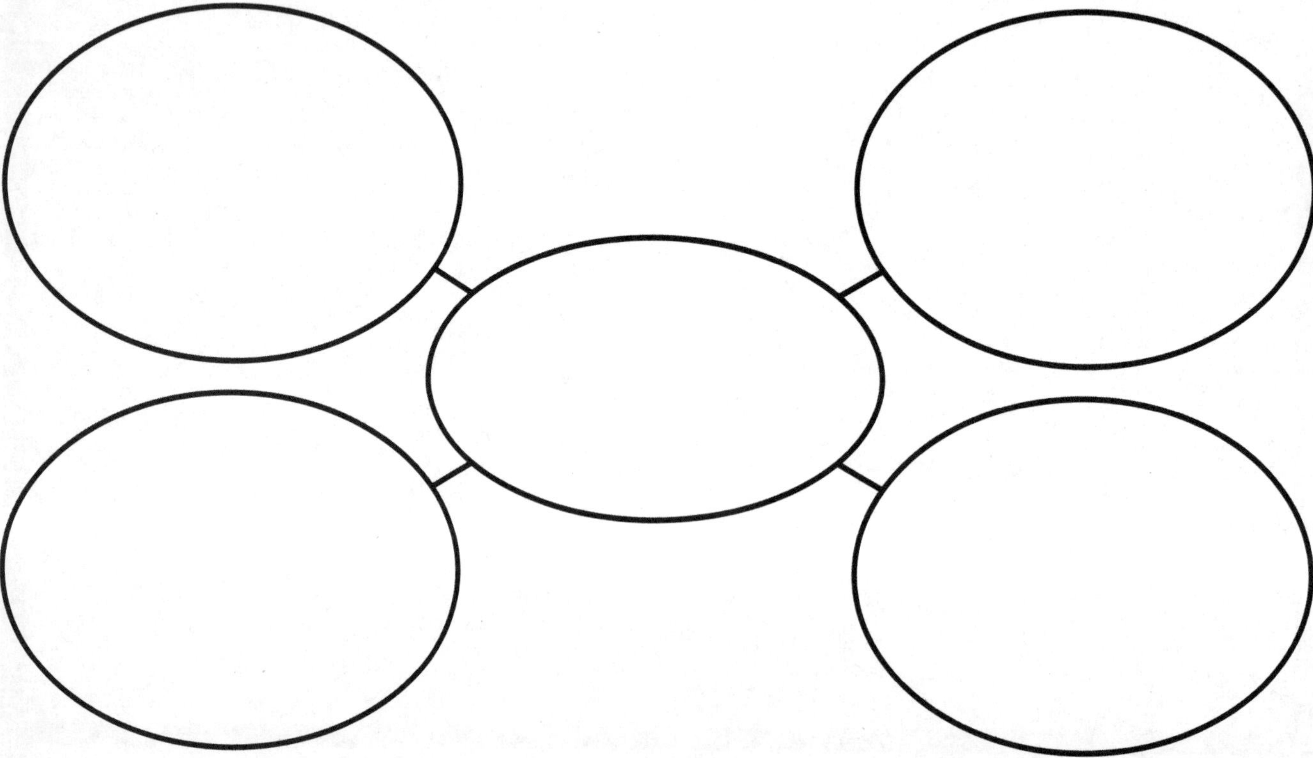

NAME ____________________

Lesson 7 The Writing Process: Persuasive Article

Now, it is time to organize the points you will make in your persuasive article. What is your strongest argument? Save that one for last. Write your important reasons or points, in these boxes. Then, number them in order.

NAME ______________________________

Lesson 7 The Writing Process: Persuasive Article

Draft

Write a first draft of your article on this page. Keep the chart on page 83 nearby. As you write, do not worry about misspelling words or getting everything perfect. Just get your ideas down in sentences and in order. Remember to give your article a title.

NAME ____________________

Lesson 7 The Writing Process: Persuasive Article

Revise

Everything that you read has been revised at least once. Even the most experienced writers look over their work and make changes. Reread your own work slowly and carefully. Then, answer the questions below about your draft. If you answer "no" to any of these questions, those are the areas that might need improvement. Feel free to make marks on your draft so you know what needs more work.

- Did you state your opinion clearly at the beginning of the article?
- Did you give strong reasons to support your opinion?
- Did you organize those reasons in a logical order, such as least important to most important?
- Did you clearly state what you want your readers to think or do?

Think carefully about your audience. With persuasive writing, it is especially important to direct your arguments at your specific audience. Ask yourself these questions.

- What opinions do my audience already hold about this issue?
- What does my audience already know about this issue?
- What will they need to know in order to understand the issue?
- What emotional appeals might sway the audience to support my opinion?

It is always a good idea to read your work out loud at the revising stage. You might hear awkward sentences or ideas that don't flow quite right. Other sentences may not say exactly what you mean.

NAME ______________________

Lesson 7 The Writing Process: Persuasive Article

Write the revision of your first draft here. As you revise, remember to keep your audience in mind.

NAME ____________________

Lesson 7 The Writing Process: Persuasive Article

Proofread

Now, correct those last little mistakes. You will be a better proofreader if you look for just one kind of error at a time. First, read for capital letters. Then, read for end punctuation, then for spelling, and so on. Use this checklist to help you as you proofread your revised persuasive article.

____ Each sentence begins with a capital letter.

____ Each sentence ends with the correct punctuation (period, question mark, or exclamation point).

____ Each sentence states a complete thought.

____ All words are spelled correctly.

When proofreaders work, they use certain symbols. These symbols will make your job easier.

- three little lines under a letter mean that the letter should be capitalized.
- Write in missing end marks like this: ⊙ ? !
- Add a comma please.
- Fix incorrect or misspelled words like these.

Use these symbols as you proofread your article. Remember to read your writing out loud, just like you did at the revising stage. You may hear mistakes or rough spots that you did not catch when reading to yourself.

Publish

Write a final copy of your article on a separate sheet of paper. Write carefully and neatly so that there are no mistakes.

Chapter 6

NAME ____________________

Lesson 1 Explanatory Writing

You hear or read explanations every day. Explanations, in the form of instructions, may come from teachers, parents, or classmates. Your teacher might explain how to answer a math problem, for example.

Explanations don't always tell how to do something. They might explain how or why something happened. For example, your teacher might explain what events led up to the signing of the Declaration of Independence, or you might read an explanation of the causes of the Revolutionary War.

List some explanations that you have read or heard this week.

Explanation	Where I Read or Heard It
____________________	____________________
____________________	____________________
____________________	____________________
____________________	____________________

Think about instructions you have read or used. How many different kinds can you list?

____________________	____________________
____________________	____________________
____________________	____________________
____________________	____________________

When you write to explain, or give instructions, you might write for these reasons:

- to tell how to make something.
- to tell how something works.
- to tell how to get somewhere.
- to tell why something happened.

NAME ____________________

Lesson 1 Explanatory Writing

Here is a simple explanation that tells how to make a bed.

First, I pull back all of the covers and smooth the bottom sheet. Then, I pull up the top sheet and straighten it. Next, I pull up the blanket nice and straight. I fold the top sheet back over the blanket about six inches. Then, I pull up the bedspread and fold it back about a foot. I fluff up the pillow and set it in place. Finally, I pull the bedspread over the pillow and make sure everything is smooth.

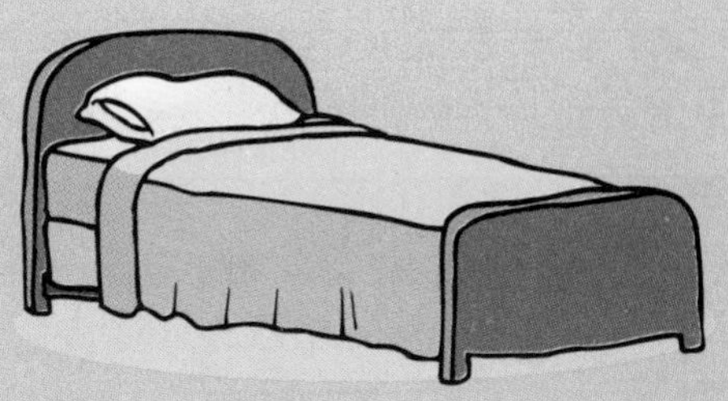

The writer stated each step in order. To help readers follow the steps, she used order words such as *first, then, next,* and *finally* to make the order very clear. Underline each of those order words that you find in the paragraph.

What do you know how to do? Write down a few simple processes, such as making a bed, that you think you could explain clearly.

____________________ ____________________

____________________ ____________________

Now, choose one of the processes you listed and think carefully about each of its steps. Imagine that you are explaining the process to someone who has never done it before. You will have to start at the very beginning. List the steps here.

Process: ____________________

Step 1: ____________________

Step 2: ____________________

Step 3: ____________________

Step 4: ____________________

Step 5: ____________________

Step 6: ____________________

Step 7: ____________________

Step 8: ____________________

Step 9: ____________________

Step 10: ____________________

Step 11: ____________________

Step 12: ____________________

Step 13: ____________________

NAME ____________________

Lesson 2 Cause-and-Effect Relationships

Why is the grass green? Why do the leaves fall? Young children often ask why. Perhaps they don't realize it, but they are looking for causes. A cause is a reason why something happens. An effect is a thing that happens. Here are some examples of causes and effects. Think about the relationship between each cause and effect.

Cause	Effect
Snow fell last night.	School was cancelled today.
The washing machine is broken.	Mom called a repairperson.
Caleb studied his spelling words.	His spelling scores improved.

When writers write to explain, they often use causes and effects. They use the words and phrases so, *because, as a result,* and *therefore* to link causes and effects. Read this paragraph about why leaves fall off in the autumn. Circle the cause-and-effect words and phrases in the paragraph.

Trees use sunlight to make a substance called chlorophyll. Chlorophyll is what gives leaves their green color. As the days get shorter, there is less light. Therefore, less chlorophyll is made. Because there is less chlorophyll, other colors in the leaves, such as yellows, oranges, and reds, are revealed.

One cause and effect from the paragraph is written for you. Write two other causes and effects.

Cause	Effect
The sun shines.	Trees make chlorophyll.

NAME ______________________

Lesson 2 Cause-and-Effect Relationships

Writers might also use causes and effects when they tell about events that happened in a story or novel.

Tony threw a red ball to his dog, Herman, but it was a little too high. The ball sailed over Herman's head, and bounced toward the haunted house at the end of the court. Herman bounded after the ball...and the house. Tony yelled for Herman to come back, but his young puppy didn't stop. Tony had no choice but to follow Herman.

Find the causes and effects in the paragraph above. Write them here. We wrote the first one for you.

Cause	Effect
Tony threw the ball too high.	The ball sailed over Herman's head.

Think about a story or novel you have read recently. What happened, and what did the characters do? Think about the events in terms of causes and effects. Ask yourself: What caused this event to happen? What effect did this event have?

Write the causes and effects of some important events from the book.

Cause	Effect

NAME ____________________

Lesson 3 News Report

In a news report, a reporter writes about an event. The event might be a car accident, a trial, or a school competition. In addition to relating events in the order in which they occurred, the reporter links causes and effects. Causes and effects help readers understand what happens and why.

Here is part of a report about a recent spelling competition. Look for words that signal cause-and-effect relationships: *so, because, as a result, therefore.* When you find them, circle them.

After weeks of practicing, the Brayton Elementary spelling team scored a victory at last night's regional spelling meet. All eight members of the team spelled each of their assigned words correctly. As a result, Brayton achieved a perfect score. The Brayton team received a lengthy ovation from the hundreds of students, teachers, and parents attending the meet because no other school had ever preformed that well at the regional level.

Andrew Carter correctly spelled *Mediterranean* to pull off Brayton's perfect score. When asked if he was worried when he got that word, he replied, "No, I wasn't, because we had studied that word especially." Brayton is a Class A school, so it will compete in next month's Class A semi-final meet.

Write two causes and two effects from the paragraph.

Cause: ____________________ Effect: ____________________

Cause: ____________________ Effect: ____________________

Cause: ____________________ Effect: ____________________

NAME ____________________

Lesson 3 News Report

Now, think about causes and effects in an event in your own life. What happened at last night's science club meeting? At basketball practice? At home last evening? Even if nothing "big" or exciting happened, there were causes and effects in action. What did you do? What happened next? What resulted from these happenings? List some events in order. Draw arrows to show any cause-and-effect relationship among events.

1. ____________________
2. ____________________
3. ____________________
4. ____________________
5. ____________________

Now, practice writing about causes and effects. Write a paragraph about the happenings you listed above. Remember to use *so, because, as a result,* and *therefore* to clarify the cause-and-effect relationships.

Lesson 4 Visual Aids

When writers write to explain, they tell how to do something, how to get somewhere, or how something works. Many explanations are more clear with the addition of a picture, map, graph, or diagram. Can you imagine putting up a tent or a canopy without a diagram to show you what to do with all the poles, ropes, and stakes?

Sometimes, a visual aid shows a great deal of information, which means the writer does not have to work so hard to explain something. Here is an example:

To test the connection between washing hands and staying healthy, we set up two test groups. Students in Group 1 washed hands twice a day. Students in Group 2 washed hands four times a day. As the graph shows, students in Group 2, who washed more frequently, had fewer absences due to colds.

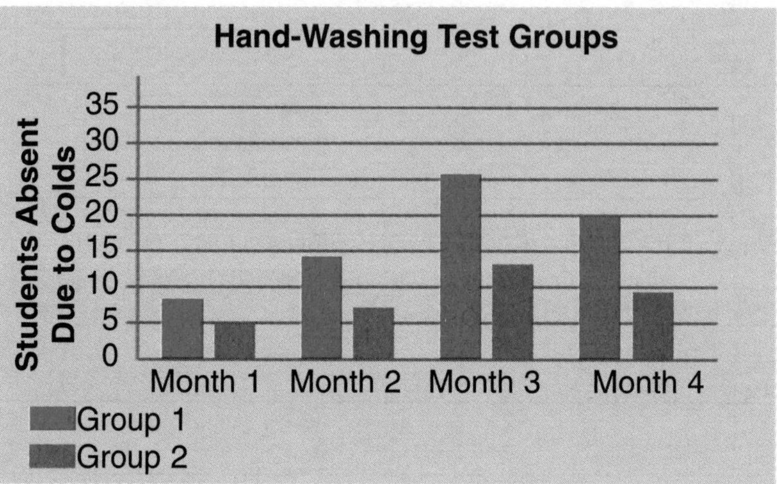

Suppose a backpack company representative is monitoring your class to see what backpack colors are most popular. First, assemble the data. List the basic colors (such as red, blue, green, yellow, purple, pink, brown, black) and make a tally mark for each backpack of that color. Then, plot your data on the graph.

Data

NAME ____________________

Lesson 4 Visual Aids

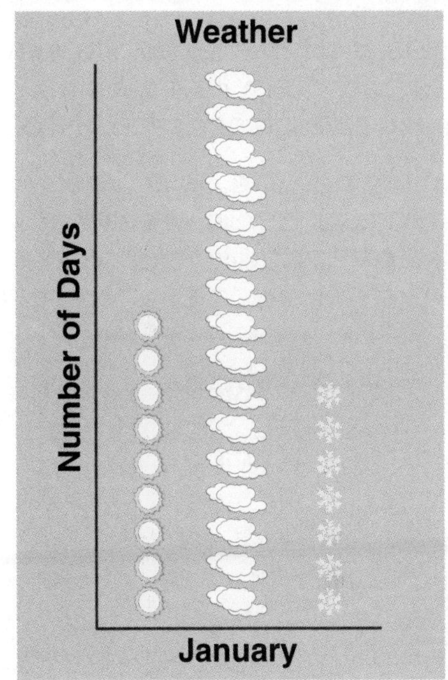

A pictograph is similar to a bar graph, but it uses symbols instead of bars to show data. Here is an example that Mrs. Halpern's class made. They kept track of the weather during each day of January. Then, at the end of the month, they made a pictograph. It shows the number of sunny days, the number of cloudy days, and the number of snowy days. Notice that you hardly need any explanation at all. The pictures do all the work.

Now, collect data for your own pictograph. You might show what kinds of pets your classmates have, what kind of trash is in your wastebasket, or the items that people eat for lunch each day. Keep in mind that the "things" you are counting should be easy to show with a simple drawing or symbol.

Data

NAME ______________________

Lesson 5 Directions

Imagine you have a new student teacher. She needs to find her way from your classroom to the main office. Can you give clear directions to help her find the way?

Directions need to be in order. As you write them, you need to think about what happens first, second, next, and so on. In addition, directions need to tell *where*. Here are some words that are often used in directions.

Direction Words	Position Words	Time-Order Words
left	over	first
right	under	second
up	past	then
down	beyond	next
north	before	after that
west	above	finally
	beside	

Here is how Carmen told the student teacher to get to the main office.

First, go out of the classroom and turn left. Go to the end of the hallway and go down the stairs on the left. Then, turn right and go past the trophy case. The office door is two doors beyond the trophy case.

What directions, positions, and time-order words do you see in Carmen's directions? Write them below.

Direction Words	Position Words	Time-Order Words
______________	______________	______________
______________	______________	______________
______________	______________	______________
______________	______________	______________

NAME ______________________

Lesson 5 Directions

Write directions that tell how to get from your classroom to the office. If you need to, close your eyes and imagine yourself walking from here to there. Now, write your directions. If you need to, look back to page 96 for direction, position, and time-order words to use.

Imagine you have been visiting Tarzan all summer. Next week, your family will arrive to visit for a few days. Then, they will take you home. They need instructions to get from the edge of the jungle to Tarzan's house. If you need to, make a sketch for yourself to plan the route. Remember to include any helpful landmarks and important sights. Then, write directions to help your family find the way.

NAME ___

Lesson 6 The Writing Process: How-to Instructions

You and your classmates have some interests that are the same and some that are different. One person really likes to play soccer, and another likes to build things out of wood. One person swims, and another makes jewelry. It is interesting to share information about each other's interests. Use the writing process to explain how to do something you enjoy.

Prewrite

Think about things that you know how to do. Maybe you know the rules of baseball or how to make a double-decker sandwich, for example. Write down some things that you know how to do.

___ ___

___ ___

___ ___

Look over your list and imagine explaining how to do each thing. With which topic are you most comfortable? Explore the idea by writing down everything you can think of about that topic. Add to this idea web as you need to.

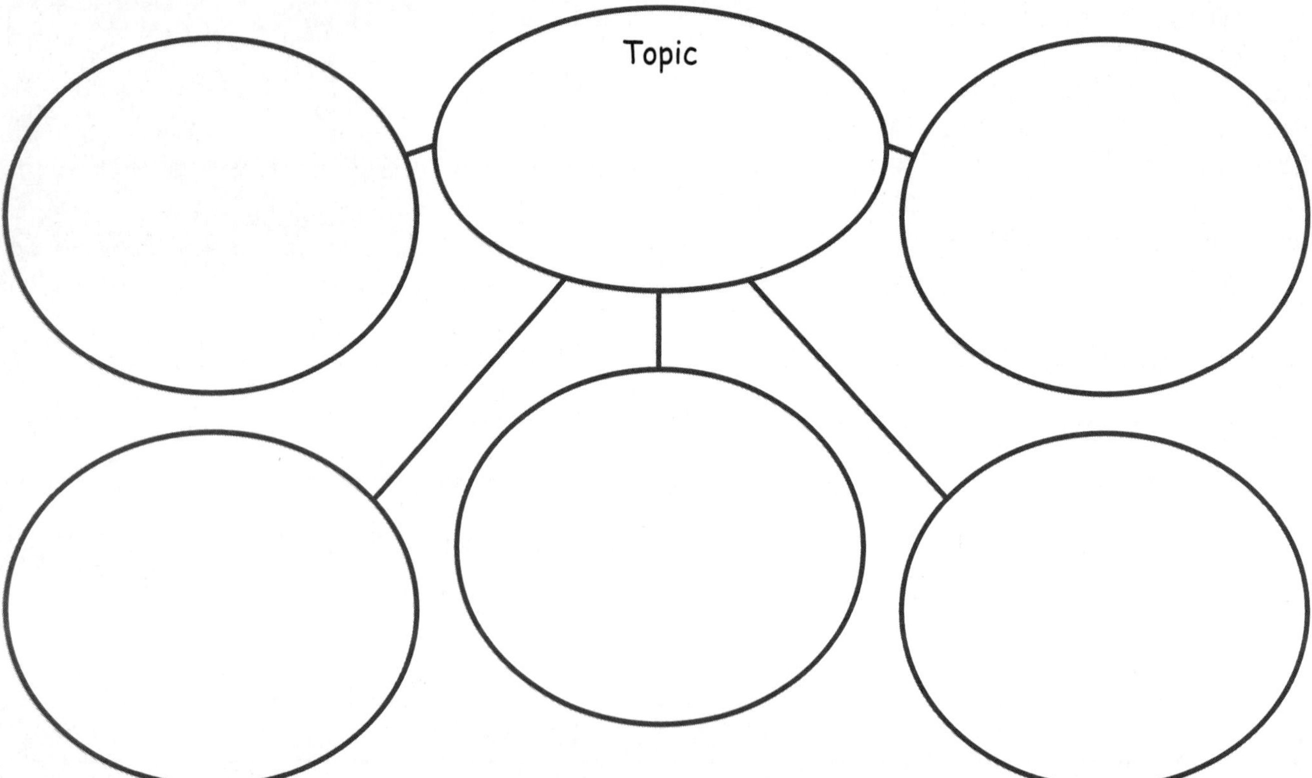

Are you still comfortable with your topic? If not, go back to your list and choose another. Explore it with an idea web on a separate sheet of paper. Remember to think about your audience. What will they need to know?

NAME ______________________________

Lesson 6 The Writing Process: How-to Instructions

Now, it is time to focus on putting ideas in order. Think about the process you are about to explain. Assume that your audience has never done this before; you need to start at the very beginning. Use the sequence chart on this page to list the important steps in your explanation. Don't worry about details at this time. Just be sure to list the main steps in the correct order.

1. ______________________________

↓

2. ______________________________

↓

3. ______________________________

↓

4. ______________________________

↓

5. ______________________________

↓

6. ______________________________

↓

7. ______________________________

↓

8. ______________________________

↓

9. ______________________________

NAME ______________________

Lesson 6 The Writing Process: How-to Instructions

Draft

Write a first draft of your instructions. Keep your sequence chart on hand as you write. Write your instructions on this page. Continue on another sheet of paper if you need to. As you write, don't worry about misspelling words or getting everything perfect. Just get your ideas down in sentences and in order.

Lesson 6 The Writing Process: How-to Instructions

Revise

Most writers feel that revising is much more difficult than writing the first draft. Try to reread your work with fresh eyes. Answer the questions below about your draft. If you answer "no" to any of these questions, those are the areas that might need improvement. Feel free to make marks on your draft so you know what needs more work. It is usually helpful to make revision notes with a different colored pen or pencil.

- Did you explain how to do something from beginning to end?
- Did you include all of the steps in order?
- Did you include time-order words to make the sequence clear?
- Did you use direction, position, and/or transition words to make your details clear?
- Did you use good describing words so your readers can "see" what they are supposed to do?
- Did you keep your audience in mind by asking yourself what they might already know or what they need to know?
- Did you include a heading or title so readers know what they are reading about?

Now, review cause-and-effect relationships.

Recognizing causes and effects helps readers understand what they are reading. The words *so, because, therefore,* and *as a result* may signal a cause-effect relationship. Here is an example:

Fold the paper in half. Press the fold firmly so the crease is sharp. Fold the paper in half the other way. Again, make a sharp crease, and unfold. Fold the paper in half diagonally, first between two corners, then between the other two. Unfold all folds. As a result, your paper should have a star-like pattern on it.

Look back at your draft and think about cause-and-effect relationships. Are the causes and effects clear? Do you need to add signal words to make them more clear?

NAME ______________________

Lesson 6 The Writing Process: How-to Instructions

Write the revision of your first draft here. As you revise, remember to think about important details that your readers will need to know.

NAME ______________________

Lesson 6 The Writing Process: How-to Instructions

Proofread

Now is the time to correct those last little mistakes. You will be a better proofreader if you look for just one kind of error at a time. Read through once for capital letters. Read again for end punctuation. Read a third time for spelling errors, and so on. Use this checklist to help you as you proofread your instructions.

____ Each sentence begins with a capital letter.

____ Each sentence ends with the correct punctuation (period, question mark, or exclamation point).

____ Each sentence states a complete thought.

____ All words are spelled correctly. (If you're not sure, check a dictionary.)

Use standard proofreading symbols as you proofread your own revised instructions.

- capitalize this letter.
- Add a missing end mark: ⊙ ? !
- Add a comma please.
- Fix incorect or misspelled words.

As you proofread, remember to read your writing out loud, even if there is no one to listen. When you read, you may hear mistakes or awkward spots that you did not see.

Publish

Write a final copy of your instructions on a separate sheet of paper. Write carefully and neatly so that there are no mistakes. If you would like, include a graph, chart, or diagram to enhance your instructions and to make them more clear. Read your instructions out loud, or perform a demonstration in front of an audience.

Chapter 7

NAME ______________________

Lesson 1 Informational Writing

In school, you have many chances to share what you know. When your teachers assign a report, they are asking you to inform them of what you know or have learned. When you write to inform, you present information about a topic.

Jason wrote a report about the North's attack on Atlanta, Georgia, during the Civil War.

Jason H.

The Fight for Atlanta

The advances of Sherman's Union troops in May of 1864 forced the Confederates to retreat into Atlanta. The entire city was ringed by earthworks. In addition, Confederate guns were positioned to fire over the earthworks at anyone who approached the city.

Faced with these strong fortifications, Sherman focused on what he felt was a weak spot. Four railroad lines led into the city. By attacking them, Sherman hoped to lure Confederate troops to fight outside the earthworks. As one of Sherman's generals, George Thomas, was positioning his troops outside the city, the Confederates saw a chance to weaken the Union army.

On July 20, John Hood led about 19,000 Confederate soldiers against the same number of Thomas's troops. The Confederates marched right into the Union gun fire. The fighting was fierce. As a result, Hood lost about 4,800 soldiers; Thomas lost about 1,800.

In spite of Hood's losses, he attacked another flank of the Union army two days later. Again, the Confederates suffered thousands more losses, and Hood retreated into Atlanta. Six days later, he tried again, and again he was defeated. Hood's aggressiveness had cost the Confederacy dearly. He was finally forced to surrender. Hood and his troops marched out of the city in silence.

NAME ____________________

Lesson 1 Informational Writing

Here are the features of informational writing:

- It provides important information about a topic.
- It presents a main idea, which is supported with facts.
- It may include information from several different sources.
- It draws a conclusion based on the information presented.
- It is organized in a logical way. Transition words connect ideas.

Why do people write to inform?

At school, you write book reports and reports about many different things. Many adults use informational writing at work. People also use informational writing in letters. In a friendly letter, you might inform the recipient about a recent family activity. In a business letter, you might inform a magazine publisher, for example, that your address has changed.

Who reads informational writing?

Everyone does. When you write at school, your teacher and your classmates are usually your audience. Remember to think about your audience as you write. What might your audience already know about the topic? What might they need or want to know?

What can informational writing be about?

You can write to inform about anything that involves facts. Informational writing often involves doing research, then telling or reporting what you know or have learned.

NAME ______________________________

Lesson 1 Informational Writing

When writers write to inform, they use transition words to connect ideas. The transition words help readers understand the connections. Here are some common transition words:

again	before long	in addition
also	but	in spite of
and	consequently	therefore
as a result	finally	thus
at the same time	for example	when
because	however	

Look back at Jason's report on page 104. Find the transition words that Jason used. Circle them.

Now, explore what you could write a report about. It is always a good idea to choose a topic in which you are interested. If you are studying the Civil War and you think battles are boring, don't choose a battle for your report topic. Choose Southern culture or the North's railroads instead. To help you think of possible topics, answer these questions.

What are some animals that interest you?

______________________ ______________________ ______________________

What are some places in the world that interest you or that you would like to visit?

______________________ ______________________ ______________________

What people from the past do you think are interesting? They might be presidents, painters, or your great-grandparents.

______________________ ______________________ ______________________

What are some interesting historical places or events that you know about? It might be an ancient city, a voyage of exploration, or a war.

______________________ ______________________ ______________________

NAME ____________________

Lesson 2 Facts, Opinions, and Bias

You already know what facts and opinions are. Facts can be proven true. Opinions are judgments that people make. What about bias?

Bias is an unfair "slant" that a writer gives to a topic. Some writers may do it by accident. Perhaps they have such strong views that they do not realize they are presenting only one point of view or only a portion of the facts. Other writers bias their work on purpose to present their own views and to persuade others to believe as they do.

Can you find the bias—the unfair slant—in this paragraph about the Civil War?

The Union troops were better equipped than the Confederate soldiers. In general, Union troops had better clothing, decent shoes, and more ammunition. It must have been humiliating for the ragged Confederate boys to see their snappy-looking counterparts. The Union soldiers, with their goal of saving the nation from the traitorous Southerners, fought proudly and with dignity.

Do you think the writer favored the Union or the Confederacy? The Union troops are described as "snappy-looking," and they fought "proudly and with dignity." The Confederate troops are described as "ragged" and as "traitorous Southerners." It is true that the Union soldiers were, generally, better equipped. Is it not also possible that they may have looked "ragged" at times, too? The Confederate soldiers also could have fought "proudly and with dignity," even if the writer doesn't believe in their cause. The writer has presented only one side of the story.

NAME ______________________________

Lesson 2 Facts, Opinions, and Bias

It is important for readers to recognize bias when they see it. Advertisements often include bias, which is one method of persuasion. News stories might contain bias, which could lead readers to misunderstand an issue or to vote for a different candidate, for example. So, it is important to think about what is fact, what is opinion, and whether all sides of an issue are being fairly presented.

As a writer, you should ask the same questions. Imagine you are reporting on a recent competition. Your school's team was competing against another school's team. It might have been a swim meet, a basketball game, or trivia quiz bowl. Both teams competed well, but your team won. Write a fair, unbiased report of the competition. Give credit to both teams for what they did well. Point out things they might have done better. Make up details as you need to.

NAME ____________________

Lesson 3 Reliable Sources

Information can be found everywhere, but which sources of information are best? How can you tell which are good and which are not good?

First, think about the kinds of information sources available. For each item, write the source that would be most useful based on the type of information required.

dictionary	**print encyclopedia**	**almanac**
newspaper	**online encyclopedia**	**Web site**
online atlas		

____________________ You want to find the date on which Abraham Lincoln delivered his Gettysburg Address.

____________________ You want to locate the boundary lines of a newly formed Russian republic.

____________________ You want to quote an announcement made by the mayor during his annual speech.

____________________ You need to understand the meaning of *deploy*.

____________________ You want to know the names of the five longest rivers in the world.

____________________ You want specific information about the architecture of Thomas Jefferson's home, Monticello.

____________________ You require current information about the number of different animal species that live on Madagascar.

You already have experience researching and finding information. Do you have some favorite sources? Write about them by completing the sentences below.

Form my school work, I usually use ____________________ because

____.

When I want information about my favorite hobby, I use ____________________

because ____.

NAME ____________________

Lesson 3 Reliable Sources

Once you find a source that seems to have the information you need, you must make sure the source is reliable. If the source is printed, ask yourself these questions:

- **When was this source published?** If you need current information, the book should be only one or two years old. Depending on the subject, even that might be too old.
- **Who wrote this book and for what purpose?** If the book is an encyclopedia, atlas, or almanac, you can be pretty confident that responsible authors wrote it to provide information. If it is a magazine article or a work of nonfiction, you need to ask more questions. Might there be bias in the material? Read the book jacket or an "About the Author" blurb in the book to discover as much as you can about the author and the purpose for writing.

If you are looking at an online source, there is a slightly different set of questions to ask. Keep in mind that anyone can create a Web site. Just because you see information on a Web site does not mean that it is accurate.

- **What person or organization established or maintains this Web site? What is the purpose of the site?** What makes this person or organization an expert on the topic?
- **What is the purpose of the site?** Whether a person or an organization maintains a site, there is the potential for bias. Does the person or organization want to inform, to sell something, or to present a certain point of view (which may or may not be biased)?
- **When was the site last updated?** Just as with print sources, the publication date may matter, depending on whether you need current information.

Write *yes* or *no* to indicate whether these sources would be reliable. Think carefully about the information given.

______ You are writing a biography of the artist John James Audubon. You go to the Audubon Web site at www.audubon.org.

______ You are writing about Thomas Jefferson's gardens at Monticello. You find a Web site maintained by a person who visited the gardens last year.

______ You are writing about hybrid cars and their impact on the environment. You consult an edition of *Car and Driver* that is a year old.

______ You are writing about all-terrain vehicles. At the library, you find a pamphlet titled "Recreation and the Outdoors." It was published by a group called *BTNN: Back to Nature—Naturally.*

NAME ______________________________

Lesson 4 Taking Notes

When you prepare a report, you will first choose a topic. Then, you will do research to locate the information you need. As you research, you must take notes on what you read. You should not write down everything you read, but only the information that is helpful for your report.

Your job is first to skim the table of contents and index to make sure the source is what you need. Then, you must read carefully. Finally, you must paraphrase, or briefly state in your own words, what you have read and record it on note cards or in a writing notebook.

Clarissa is writing a report on farming in the 1800s. Here is one of her note cards.

This is the **topic**. → Changes in Farming

These are the **notes**.
1834
reaper, by Cyrus McCormick
harvested grain
replaced hand scythe

This is the **source**. → Life in Nineteenth-Century America, page 89

Clarissa's note card has three important parts. First, at the top she listed the topic. She knows that one part of her report will be about changes in farming. She marks each note card with a specific topic. Labeling the cards in that way will make organizing them and writing her draft much easier.

Second, she wrote her notes. They are very brief. She included only the most important pieces of information.

Finally, she wrote the name of the source and the page number. If she needs to go back and check a fact or get more information, she can do so easily.

NAME ____________________

Lesson 4 Taking Notes

Clarissa's classmate, Bart, is writing a report on George Washington. He knows that his report will have sections about Washington's childhood, his early career, his presidential years, and his later life. Find an article about Washington's life in a print or online source. Then, take some notes for Bart. Label each card with one of the sections, listed above. Remember to keep your notes brief, and to list your source at the bottom of each card.

NAME ______________________

Lesson 5 The Writing Process: Informational Writing

Writing a report is a good way to show what you know. It is also a good way to learn something new. Use the writing process to plan and write a report.

Prewrite

Look back at the topic ideas you recorded on page 106. Choose one and begin to explore that topic with the help of this chart.

Topic: ______________________

What I Know	What I Want to Know	How or Where I Might Find Out

If you are comfortable with this subject, research it and take notes. Remember to organize your note cards by specific subject. For example, if you are writing about river otters, you might organize your note cards in these categories: description, habitat, food, and interesting facts.

NAME ________________

Lesson 5 The Writing Process: Informational Writing

Now, it is time to focus on putting ideas in order. Think about your topic. How should you organize information? By time order? By cause and effect? In order of importance? Looking at and organizing your note cards might help you decide. List your main points or ideas below. Then, number them in the order you will use them.

Name of Subject: ________________

NAME ______________________

Lesson 5 The Writing Process: Informational Writing

Draft

It is time to write a first draft of your report. Keep your notes and the chart on page 114 nearby as you write. Write your draft on this page. Continue on another sheet of paper if you need to. As you write, don't worry about misspelling words or getting everything perfect. Just get your ideas down in sentences and paragraphs.

NAME ______________________

Lesson 5 The Writing Process: Informational Writing

Revise

Every writer can improve his or her work. Pick up your report and read it as if you are seeing it for the first time. Remember, even experienced writers feel that revising is much more difficult than writing the first draft.

Answer the questions below about your draft. If you answer "no" to any of these questions, those are the areas that might need improvement. Feel free to make marks on your draft, so you know what needs more work.

- Did you present information clearly and in a logical order?
- Does each paragraph consist of a main idea supported by facts?
- Did you include transition words to connect ideas?
- Did you begin with a sentence that will make readers want to keep reading?
- Did you use information from several different sources?
- Did you draw a conclusion based on the information presented?
- Did you keep your audience in mind by asking yourself what they might already know or what they need to know?
- Did you present a fair or balanced view of the subject?

Here are a few pointers about making your report interesting to read.

- Vary the length of your sentences. Mixing short, medium, and long sentences keeps your readers interested.
- Vary the style of your sentences. Begin sentences with different kinds of words or clauses. For example, begin some sentences with verbs, some with phrases (such as "After the war" or "In spite of the war"), and some with clauses (such as "While Jefferson was in France,").
- Do not use first-person pronouns in your report. For example, do not write, "I am writing a report on skateboarding." Also, do not write, "According to the statistics I found, skateboarding is more popular with boys than girls." In this case, delete the words *I found.*

On page 117, write the revision of your draft. As you revise, pay special attention to the length and style of your sentences.

NAME ______________________

Lesson 5 The Writing Process: Informational Writing

NAME ______________________

Lesson 5 The Writing Process: Informational Writing

Proofread

Now, correct those last little mistakes. Proofreading is easier if you look for just one kind of error at a time. So, read through once looking for capital letters. Read again for end punctuation. Read a third time for spelling errors, and so on. Use this checklist as you proofread your report.

____ Each sentence begins with a capital letter.

____ Each sentence ends with the correct punctuation (period, question mark, or exclamation point).

____ Each sentence states a complete thought.

____ All proper nouns begin with capital letters.

____ All words are spelled correctly.

Use standard proofreading symbols as you proofread your revised report.

- capitalize this letter.
- Add a missing end mark: ⊙ ? !
- Add a comma please.
- Fix incorect or misspelled words.

Remember to read your writing out loud during the proofreading stage. You may hear a mistake or rough spot that you did not see.

Publish

Write a final copy of your report on page 119. Write carefully and neatly so that there are no mistakes. Make a cover that includes a drawing or a picture that relates to your topic. Read your report out loud to the class.

NAME ______

Lesson 5 The Writing Process: Informational Writing

NAME ______________________

Writer's Handbook

Writing Basics

Sentences are a writer's building blocks. To be a good writer, one must first be a good sentence writer. A sentence always begins with a capital letter.

He walked around the block.

A sentence must always tell a complete thought. It has a subject and a predicate.

Complete Sentence: He lives around the corner.
Incomplete Sentence: The block where he lives.

A sentence always ends with an end mark. There are three kinds of end marks. A sentence that tells something ends with a period.

He walked around the block**.**

A sentence that asks something ends with a question mark.

Did he walk around the block**?**

A sentence that shows excitement or fear ends with an exclamation point.

He ran all the way around the block**!**

Punctuation can be a writer's road map.

End marks on sentences show whether a sentence is a statement, a question, or an exclamation.

Commas help keep ideas clear.

In a list or series: I saw sea stars**,** crabs**,** and seals at the beach.
In a compound sentence: I wanted a closer look**,** but the crab crawled away.
After an introductory phrase or clause: Later that day**,** a storm blew up.
To separate a speech tag: I called to Mom**,** "It's really getting windy!"
"I hope it doesn't rain**,**" she said.

Quotation marks show the exact words that a speaker says. Quotation marks enclose the speaker's words and the punctuation marks that go with the words.

"Does it matter?**"** Neil remarked. **"**We're already wet.**"**
"I'd rather be wet from below than from above,**"** said Dad.
"Be careful!**"** Mom yelled. **"**Those waves are getting big!**"**

Writer's Handbook

The Writing Process

When writers write, they take certain steps. Those steps make up the writing process.

Step 1: Prewrite

First, writers choose a topic. Then, they collect and organize ideas or information. They might write their ideas in a list or make a chart and begin to put their ideas in some kind of order.

Mariko is going to write about her neighborhood. She put her ideas in a web.

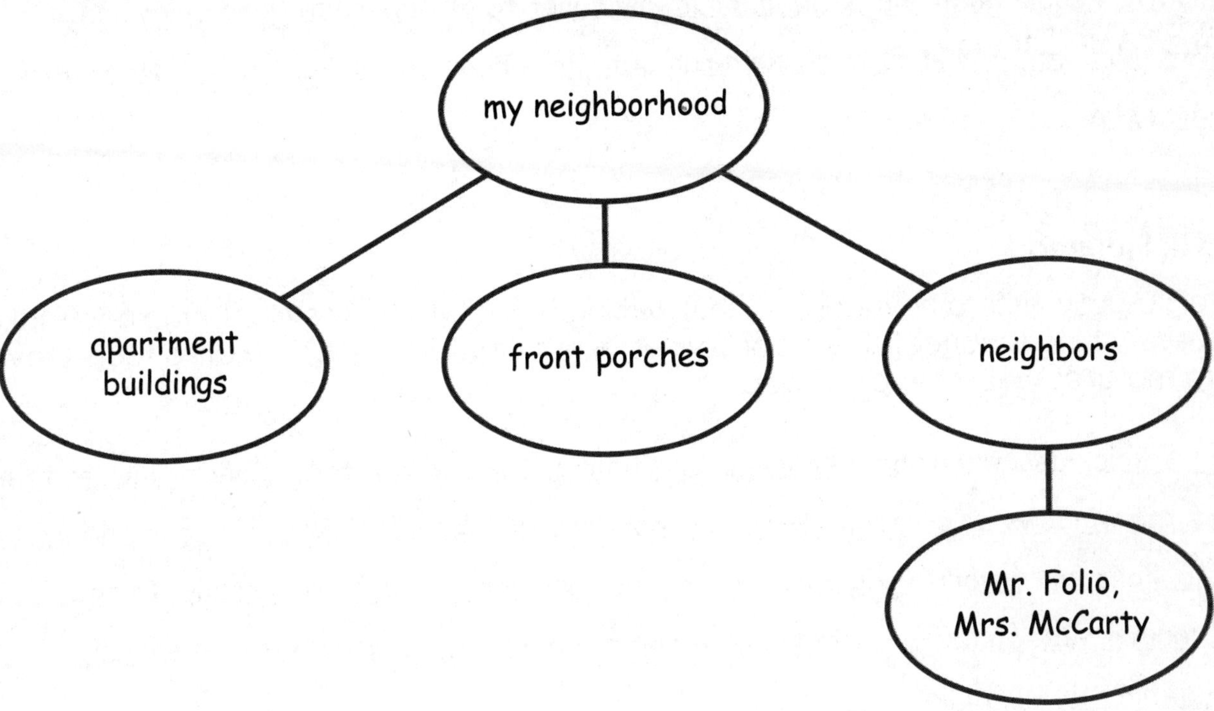

Step 2: Draft

Next, writers put their ideas on paper in a first draft. Writers know that there might be mistakes in this first draft. That's okay. Here is Mariko's first draft.

> Brick apartment houses are all around me. I live in tallest one. Across the street is the shortest. I like to think of the windows as eyes. and the front porches are the mouths People go in and out. Mr. Folio, my favorite neighbor, sits and sings songs. Mrs. McCarty pretends to shake a rug out the window but she is really listening to Mr. Folio.

NAME ____________________

Writer's Handbook

Step 3: Revise

Then, writers change or fix their first draft. They might decide to move ideas around, add information, or take out words or sentences that don't belong. Here are Mariko's changes.

the
Brick apartment houses are all around me. I live in ^ tallest one. ~~Across the street is the shortest.~~ I like to think of the windows as eyes. and the front porches are the
on his porch Italian
mouths People go in and out. Mr. Folio, my favorite neighbor, sits ^ and sings ^ songs.
In the evening,
^ Mrs. McCarty pretends to shake a rug out the window but she is really listening to Mr. Folio.

Step 4: Proofread

Writers usually write a new copy so their writing is neat. Then, they look again to make sure everything is correct. They look for mistakes in their sentences. Mariko found several more mistakes when she proofread her work.

Brick apartment houses are all around me. I live in the tallest one. I like to think
as
of the windows as eyes/and ~~the~~ front porches ^ ~~are the~~ mouths. People go in and out. Mr. Folio, my favorite neighbor, sits on his porch and sings Italian songs. In the evening, Mrs. McCarty pretends to shake a rug out the ^ window but she is really listening to Mr. Folio.

Step 5: Publish

Finally, writers make a final copy that has no mistakes. They might choose to add pictures and create a book. Then, they are ready to publish their writing. They might choose to read their writing out loud or have a friend read it.

Writer's Handbook

Personal Narrative

In a personal narrative, a writer writes about something she has done or seen. It might tell about something funny, sad, or unusual. A personal narrative can be about anything, as long as the writer is telling about one of his or her own experiences. Here is the final version of Mariko's paragraph about her neighborhood.

Describing words help readers "see" or "hear" what is happening.

A time word tells when something happens.

Brick apartment houses are all around me. I live in the tallest one. I like to think of the windows as eyes and front porches as mouths. People go in and out. Mr. Folio, my favorite neighbor, sits on his porch and sings Italian songs. In the evening, Mrs. McCarty pretends to shake a rug out the window, but she is really listening to Mr. Folio.

The words *me* and *I* show that the writer is part of the action.

The writer stayed on topic. All of the sentences give information about Mariko's neighborhood.

Stories

Writers write about made-up things. They might write about people or animals. The story might seem real, or it might seem fantastic, or unreal. Here is a story that Mariko wrote. It has both human and animal characters in it. The animals speak, so Mariko's story is not realistic.

The story has a beginning, a middle, and an end.

Sensory words help readers visualize what is happening.

The story includes dialogue, or conversation among characters.

In the Neighborhood

It is nearly sunrise, and the neighborhood is waking up. Windows glow where the early birds prepare breakfast. Bacon sizzles in the Hooper kitchen, and the smell draws a hungry crowd.

In the corner, eight furry paws scramble through the crack between the wall and the baseboard. They pause at the corner of the wastebasket, then scamper to the refrigerator. Blue fuzzy slippers come quickly forward and stamp on the floor. "Go away, you critters!" The critters huddle deeper in the darkness. Four black eyes watch for crumbs to fall. Two long tails twitch with excitement.

Mrs. Hooper's slippers scuff across the floor. "It's ready!" she calls upstairs. In a moment, Mr. Hooper's heavy work boots thump down the stairs. *Scuff-thump*, *Scuff-thump*, the people go into the other room.

"Now, it's our turn," smiles Velvet.

Her brother Flannel nods and shrugs. "It's a dirty job, but someone has to do it." And he and his sister go to work, clearing the floor of crumbs.

The first paragraph establishes the setting.

Time and order words keep ideas in order.

This story is written in third-person point of view. So, words such as *he, she, her, his,* and *they* refer to the characters.

NAME ______________________

Writer's Handbook

Descriptive Writing

When writers describe, they might tell about an object, a place, or an event. They use sensory words so that readers can see, hear, smell, feel, or taste whatever is being described. In this example of descriptive writing, Mariko compared her old bedroom with her new bedroom.

The writer uses the whole-to-whole comparison method. She describes one whole room in the first paragraph, and the other room in the second paragraph.

My bedroom in our old apartment was green. It was a nice grassy green, and it always made me think of a forest. My bed was in the left corner, between the two windows. The wall straight ahead was almost all shelves, where I kept my turtle collection, my books, and all my other stuff. My yellow beanbag chair and the closet were on the right side of the room.

My new bedroom is blue. I like to think of it as sky blue. On the left side of the room is one big window. I put my beanbag chair right beside the window. Straight ahead is my bed. On the right is a built-in bookshelf and the closet door.

Sensory details help readers visualize the scene.

The writer organizes details from side to side. She first tells what is on the left, then straight ahead, then on the right.

Informational Writing

When writers write to inform, they present information about a topic. Informational writing is nonfiction. It is not made up; it contains facts.

Mariko interviewed her neighbor, Mr. Folio. Then, she wrote about what she learned. Here is one of her paragraphs.

Mariko states her main idea in a topic sentence. It is the first sentence of the paragraph.

My neighbor, Mr. Folio, has lived in the same apartment building all his life. His parents and his grandparents lived there, too. In fact, his grandparents were the first people to move into the building in 1921. He remembers his grandmother telling about how new and shiny the doorknobs and the stair railings were. Mr. Folio's grandparents lived on the top floor because his grandfather liked the view. Later, his parents lived on the fourth floor because that was what was available at the time. Now, Mr. Folio lives on the first floor. He says he likes to see what is going on in the neighborhood.

These sentences contain details that support the main idea.

Transition words connect ideas.

Writer's Handbook

Explanatory (or How-to) Writing

Writers explain how to do things. They might write about how to play a game, create an art project, or follow a recipe. Mariko has written instructions for a marble game that she plays with her sister.

The steps are all in order, starting with the items needed to play the game.

Order words help readers keep the steps in order.

Mariko's Marbles

First, you need 20 small marbles, two shooter marbles, and someone to play with. Choose a square of sidewalk that doesn't have very many cracks or bumps in it. Roll the small marbles onto the square. Then, players take turns using their shooters to try to knock marbles out of the square. Each player gets two tries per turn. Players may knock out only one marble at a time. If a player knocks out more than one marble, the player must put back all of her knocked-out marbles. Finally, when all 20 marbles have been knocked out of the square, the player with the most marbles is the winner.

Clear words help readers understand the instructions.

Persuasive Writing

In persuasive writing, writers try to make readers think, feel, or act in a certain way. Persuasive writing shows up in newspaper and magazine articles, letters to the editor, business letters, and in advertisements, of course. Mariko's mom has written a letter to the editor of the local newspaper.

The writer begins by stating some opinions.

The writer uses an emotional appeal to persuade readers to agree with her.

Dear Editor:

I used to be proud of my neighborhood. The streets used to look nice, and people cared about keeping them that way. Now, however, the sidewalks on 41st Street are terribly cracked and broken, and the city has no plans to fix them. In some places, it is not even safe to walk. The older people in the neighborhood have to walk in the street to get to the grocery store. Can't the city repair the sidewalks? It would feel good to be proud and safe in my neighborhood again.

F. Torunaga

The writer states some facts to lend support to her opinions.

The writer includes a specific request for action.

NAME ____________________

Writer's Handbook

Friendly Letters

Writers write friendly letters to people they know. They might share news or ideas or request information. A friendly letter has five parts: the date, the greeting, the body, the closing, and the signature. Here is a letter Mariko wrote to her grandfather.

Each word in the greeting begins with a capital letter.

There is always a comma after the person's name.

The date is in the upper, right corner.

September 2

Dear Grandfather,

We are all settled in our new apartment. I love my new bedroom. Dad says we can even paint some white puffy clouds on the ceiling. Then it really will seem like a sky-blue room.

I like the neighbors, so far. Mr. Folio is my favorite. He lives in a building across the street. When there's nothing to do, I go sit on his front steps and visit. He can tell a story about almost everyone who passes by on the sidewalk.

I think you would like Mr. Folio. When are you and Grandmother going to come and visit? Soon, I hope.

Love as always,
Mariko

The body of the letter gives information.

Only the first word of the closing begins with a capital letter. There is always a comma after the closing.

The writer signs his or her name.

NAME ____________________

Writer's Handbook

Business Letters

Writers write business letters to people or organizations with whom they are not familiar. Business letters usually involve a complaint or a request for information. Mariko needs information for a school report. She wrote a business letter to request information.

The heading includes the sender's address and the date.

764 41st Street
Indianapolis, IN 46208
October 5, 2007

The inside address is the name and address of the recipient.

Monroe County Historical Society
202 E. 6th Street
Bloomington, IN 47402

Dear Monroe County Historical Society:

The greeting is followed by a colon.

The text of the letter is the body.

My class is studying state history this year. Each of us has chosen a county to study. I chose Monroe County because my grandparents live there.

On your Web site, I saw that you have a free pamphlet titled "Monroe County: Through the Years." Please send me one copy of that brochure. I have included an envelope with postage.

Thank you for your help with my report.

Sincerely,

The closing is followed by a comma.

The sender always includes a signature.

Mariko Torunaga
Mariko Torunaga

Answer Key

Chapter 1

Lesson 1

Page 5
Circled sentence: Fishing requires certain equipment.
Details will vary.

Page 6
Main ideas and details will vary.
Paragraphs will vary.

Lesson 2

Page 7
Underlined topic sentence: My dad was always happy when he was fishing.
Possible topic sentence: Lantern Lake is the source of many fishing tales.
Details will vary.

Page 8
Underlined topic sentence: His pleasure came from fishing, not from catching fish.
Details will vary.
Underlined main idea: Water safety takes some extra thought.
Details will vary.

Page 9
Paragraphs will vary.

Lesson 3

Page 10
astronaut
Main ideas will vary.

Page 11
Underlined topic sentence: The courthouse in our city is made of great big limestone blocks.
Crossed-out sentence: Beside the old quarry is where the first mayor lived.
Details will vary.
Underlined topic sentence: Long ago, people built their homes with whatever was handy.
Crossed-out sentence: I was in a log cabin once, and it was made out of huge logs.
Details will vary.

Lesson 4

Page 13
Order of steps shown:
Step 3: Revise
Step 5: Publish
Step 1: Prewrite
Step 2: Draft
Step 4: Proofread

Lesson 5

Page 14
instructions—to explain
letter to the editor—to persuade
retold fairy tale—to entertain
article—to inform

Lesson 6

Page 15
Suggestions may include simplifying language, making the writing more interesting, explaining the steps more fully, and including illustrations.

Lesson 7

Page 16
Prewriting notes will vary.

Page 17
Paragraphs will vary.

Chapter 2

Lesson 1

Page 19
Notes will vary.

Lesson 2

Page 20
Listed words will vary.
Sentences will vary.

Page 21
Circled transition words: *During, As soon as, When, Then*
Sentences will vary.

Lesson 3

Page 23
<u>Jacob</u> pitched well.
Some <u>fans</u> were showing poor sportsmanship.
X The <u>team</u> was coached well.
X The opening <u>pitch</u> was thrown by the mayor.
Sentences will vary.
Paragraphs will vary.

Lesson 4

Page 24
Ideas and idea webs will vary.

Page 25
Entries in sequence charts will vary.

Page 26
Drafts will vary.

Page 28
Revisions will vary.

Chapter 3

Lesson 1

Page 30
Details will vary.

Page 31
Paragraphs will vary.

Lesson 2

Page 32
Revised sentences will vary.

Page 33
Revised sentences will vary.

Lesson 3

Page 34
Descriptive paragraphs will vary.

Page 35
Details and descriptive paragraphs will vary.

Lesson 4

Page 37
Friendly letters will vary.

Lesson 5

Page 38
Circled spatial words: *down, high, below, below, around, across*

Page 39
Spatial descriptions will vary.

Lesson 6

Page 40
Entries in Venn diagrams will vary.

Page 41
Entries in Venn diagrams will vary.
Sentences will vary.

Lesson 7

Page 42
Sam is happier than Alex
Cal is more confused than Sam.
Alex is sadder than Cal.

Page 43
Comparative forms to be used in sentences: *biggest, heaviest, safest, most exciting*

Lesson 8

Page 44
Details in Venn diagrams will vary.

Page 45
Comparison paragraphs will vary.

Lesson 9

Page 46
Setting ideas will vary.
Entries in idea webs will vary.

Page 47
Methods of organization and paragraphs will vary.

Page 48
Revisions will vary.

Page 49
Published descriptive paragraphs will vary.

Answer Key

Chapter 4

Lesson 1

Page 52
Characters: Della, Dean
Setting: in a city, on a porch, and on a sidewalk
Setting words from story: buildings, sidewalks, porch
Problem: The children are hot and trying to cool down.
Solution: She finds an open fire hydrant.
Possible dialogue: "It's so hot,..." OR "Let's go out on the porch."
Dean admires his sister. The narrator tells us that he "usually liked Della's ideas."
Sense words: *shrugged, heat, oven, shady, cold river*

Lesson 2

Page 53
She seems bored or distracted.
He or she has been earning money by collecting aluminum cans. He or she wants to deposit money into the bank.

Page 54
"Here is your deposit slip," said the teller.
I took it and said, "Thank you, ma'am."
"Do you need anything else?" she asked.
Dialogue will vary.

Page 55
Sentences will vary.

Lesson 3

Page 56
Responses to Doyle passage:
The characters are travelling through the countryside, only occasionally passing a house. The driver has a whip, so they must be in a horse-drawn carriage. There is a building in the distance. It is called *Baskerville Hall*, and it has two high, narrow towers.
Mood: bleak, harsh
Possible "happy" setting details:
Weather: sunny day
Time of day: dawn, morning, afternoon, evening
Places: at home; in a familiar place; in a fresh, outdoor setting

Page 57
Possible "scary" setting details:
Weather: raining, stormy, cloudy
Time of day: evening, after dark, midnight
Places: in an unfamiliar place; in a dark place; in an abandoned or run-down place
Paragraphs will vary.

Lesson 4

Page 58
Characters and details will vary.

Page 59
Character details and paragraphs will vary.

Lesson 5

Page 61
Responses will vary.

Lesson 6

Page 62
Character ideas will vary.

Page 63
Character ideas will vary.

Lesson 7

Page 64
Entries in idea webs will vary.

Page 65
Story maps will vary.

Chapter 4 continued

Page 66
Drafts will vary.

Page 68
Revisions will vary.

Chapter 5

Lesson 1

Page 71
Persuasive articles will vary.

Lesson 2

Page 72
Circled opinion signal words: *believe, think*

Page 73
Ms. Whitaker's article:
The first two paragraphs of the article contain many facts that students may cite.
Opinions:
The students return to the classroom more ready to learn.
The new system is great.

Akira's article:
Possible facts:
Akira ate lunch in 6 minutes. He raced with a friend. He eats bigger lunches now.
Circled opinion signal words: *thinks, think*
Possible opinions:
Recess is more fun than lunch. Akira is growing. Lunch is okay.
Students' personal opinions will vary.

Lesson 3

Page 74
Issues will vary.

Page 75
The emotional appeal in Mr. Devon's letter tries to get at strong feelings that people have about children being allowed to do fun things, such as exercising and playing with friends.
Letters to editor will vary.

Chapter 5 continued

Lesson 4

Page 76
The sock slogan appeals to our need to feel good and comfortable.
The eyeglass slogan appeals to our need to fit in with other people.
parents, grandparents, other relatives
Possible response: I would need to appeal to their strong feelings about keeping babies warm and comfortable and safe.

Page 77
Slogans and advertisements will vary.

Lesson 5

Page 78
Reasons why people should donate food:
1) The class that collects the most cans will earn book fair coupons.
2) All canned goods collected will go to the Fourth Street Food Pantry.
3) The Fourth Street Food Pantry provides food to approximately 60 families.
4) In the winter, that number nearly doubles.
5) These families rely on the Food Pantry to keep themselves fed and healthy.

Page 79
Prewriting notes and letters will vary.

Lesson 6

Page 81
Letters of request will vary.

Lesson 7

Page 82
Students' ideas for improvements will vary.
Entries in idea webs will vary.

Page 83
Students' organizational notes will vary.

Page 84
Drafts will vary.

Page 86
Revisions will vary.

Answer Key

Chapter 6

Lesson 1

Page 88
Responses will vary.

Page 89
Order words underlined in paragraph: *First, Then, Next, Then, Finally*
Responses will vary.

Lesson 2

Page 90
Possible causes and effects:
Cause: Days get shorter. Effect: There is less light.
Cause: There is less light. Effect: Less chlorophyll is made.
Cause: There is less chlorophyll in leaves. Effect: Other leaf colors show.

Page 91
Possible causes and effects:
Cause: The ball sailed over Herman's head. Effect: It bounced toward the haunted house.
Cause: The ball bounced toward the haunted house. Effect: Herman bounded toward the house.
Cause: Herman bounded toward the house. Effect: Tony followed Herman.
Responses will vary.

Lesson 3

Page 92
Circled words in paragraph: *As a result, because, so*
Possible causes and effects:
Cause: The team practiced for weeks. Effect: The team won the spelling meet.
Cause: All team members spelled their words correctly. Effect: The team scored a perfect score.
Cause: Brayton scored a perfect score. Effect: They received a lengthy ovation.
Cause: Brayton won the regional spelling meet. Effect: Brayton will go on to the semi-final meet.

Page 93
Responses will vary.
Paragraphs will vary.

Lesson 4

Page 94
Bar graphs will vary.

Page 95
Pictographs will vary.

Lesson 5

Page 96
Direction Words: *First, out, left, end, down, left, Then, right, past, beyond*
Position Words: *out, end, past, beyond*
Time-Order Words: *first, Then*

Page 97
Directions will vary.

Lesson 6

Page 98
Responses will vary.

Page 99
Entries in chart will vary.

Page 100
Instructions will vary.

Page 102
Revisions will vary.

Chapter 7

Lesson 1

Page 106
Circled transition words (in text on page 104): *In addition, As, As a result, In spite of, Again, later, again, finally*
Topic explorations will vary.

Lesson 2

Page 108
Responses will vary.

Lesson 3

Page 109
print encyclopedia
online atlas
newspaper
dictionary
almanac
web site
online encyclopedia
Sentences will vary.

Page 110
yes
no
no
no

Lesson 4

Page 112
Entries on note cards will vary.

Lesson 5

Page 113
Entries in chart will vary.

Page 114
Entries in chart will vary.

Page 115
Drafts will vary.

Page 117
Revisions will vary.

Page 119
Published reports will vary.